THE COURAGE TO BE KIND

To God – The core of kindness.
My Family—The kindest gift I have ever received.
My Parents—Your kindness can never be repaid.
My Siblings—Our parents would be proud.
And, to those who seek the "Courage to be Kind."

THE COURAGE TO BE KIND

J. TOUCHÉ

The Courage to Be Kind Copyright © 2024 by J. Touché

All rights reserved. No part of this book may be used or reproduced in any manner whatsoever without the author's written permission except in the case of brief quotations embodied in critical articles and reviews.

The information in this book is distributed on an "as is" basis, without warranty. Although every precaution has been taken in the preparation of this work, neither the author nor the publisher shall have any liability to any person or entity with respect to any loss or damage caused or alleged to be caused directly or indirectly by the information contained in this book.

Paperback ISBN: 978-1-959681-57-1
eBook ISBN: 978-1-959681-58-8
Hardcover ISBN: 978-1-959681-59-5
Library of Congress Number: Pending

Photo Credit Author Headshot: Alex Marie
Cover and Interior Design by Ann Aubitz
Published by Kirk House Publishers

Kirk House Publishers
1250 E 115th Street
Burnsville, MN 55337
612-781-2815
kirkhousepublishers.com

A SPECIAL THANKS TO

Rev. Reginald E. Stevens, MDiv, MRE, MHS—My mentor.

Mr. Harris Rosen and Ms. Mary Deatrick, Rosen Hotels and Resorts, Orlando, Florida, for their commitment to kindness and permission to include *The Mr. Harris Rosen Story* in this book.

James O. Prochaska, PhD, University of Rhode Island, for rendering his permission (cocreator) to use the *Transtheoretical Model of Behavior Change* in this book.

Dacher Keltner, PhD, Codirector of the Greater Good Science Center, University of California, Berkeley.

Animal Legal Defense Fund (aldf.org)

CONTENTS

	Prologue	11
1	What is courage?	15
2	What is kindness?	17
3	Why having courage and kindness is essential for change	19
4	Personal struggles with kindness	21
5	When kindness is not "stuff"	23
6	Why some fear being kind	29
7	When others use or abuse your kindness	40
8	"Goody two-shoes," Why are you such a threat?	42
9	Kind or nice? Do not let others change you!	44
10	Bitterness is the enemy of kindness	48
11	Assertiveness is essential to being courageous and kind	50
12	What kindness is not; it is not all nice!	52
13	Can anyone be kind? Can we change? The challenge of "reprogramming" our kindness	57
14	The future of kindness	60
15	Kindness and technology	63

16	Kids and kindness	65
17	You were born out of kindness	72
18	How kindness went to the sidelines	75
19	The curse of kindness?	81
20	Discernment and kindness	83
21	What is your kind IQ?	88
22	Visualization and kindness	90
23	Prayer, faith, and kindness	91
24	Oh, goodness!	95
25	Kindness and health	97
26	Why kindness should be our legacy	99
27	Kindness: our environment and other species	102
28	Kindness and attitude	104
29	When kindness and enabling bisect—having the courage and wisdom to act	108
30	Kindness, love, and respect	111
31	Wounded people and kindness	115
32	Kindness, race, and ethnicity	117
	Cousins of kindness	120
	Cousins of courage	120
33	Why we must not give up on being kind	121
34	You cannot 'save the world' through your kindness!	124
35	Kindness is like a garden	126
36	Courage or cowardice?	128
37	Can you be too kind?	130
38	Have you ever missed an opportunity to show kindness?	132
39	Take time to say, "Thank you," when you are shown kindness	135

40	Perhaps, some of the greatest examples of courage and kindness	137
41	When kind acts beget kindness in return	139
42	Kindness and religion	142
43	It takes courage to be kind when we are hurting	144
44	Kindness: Your kids and your parents	147
45	Excuses for not showing kindness	149
46	Kindness and our enemies	151
47	Kindness and friends	153
48	Kindness and forgiveness	155
49	Why random acts of kindness should start at home	157
50	Kindness and our neighbors	159
51	The many faces of kindness	162
52	Kindness and community	164
	In conclusion	166
	Seek the Courage to Be Kind	168
	Notes	169
	About the Author	172

PROLOGUE

We are all seekers in this life, and as such, are given gifts and talents which The Creator left up to each of us to discover for ourselves. In every author there is a novel; in every artist—a masterpiece, in every musician—a "classic" song, in every doctor—a cure, in every mortician—a memory, in every parent—a future, in every theologian—a message, and in every seeker—a meaning. Regardless of one's gifts or talents, we can all aspire to seek and show kindness to others. To effect change, kindness must be married with courage; for what is being kind without the courage to show that you care? When you show that you are concerned about the well-being of others, you expose a very vulnerable side of yourself, the compassionate, loving, altruistic part that most fight to protect or shield rather than give away.

This is where courage will be needed because these same virtues and values are the ones that can move both man and mountain. I do not need to tell you that we are living in some very challenging times and that humans are at a crossroad in terms of our existence. While I will not confess to having any esoteric knowledge about all the events that are shaping our lives, I do see an increased decline in our civility overall as well as our capacity to show human kindness. I have seen a spirit of meanness sweep across our nation and the world, as many of you have. Maybe, it has always been present and through social media, television, the internet, blogs, and other communications it brings this ugliness to us almost immediately. It concerned me enough, based on conversations that I have had with people whom I met during my travels, or worked with, or worshiped with, or things that I have experienced or sensed daily, national and local news stories, and blogs and online forums I have participated in; that a book was needed to help sort through all that we have learned about kindness—what it is and what it is not.

While there are many fine books available that speak of kindness, when I first started writing my book in 2013, I had not read one that talked in detail about the courage it takes to be kind, or how this relates to various aspects of the human condition. I wanted to approach kindness primarily in layman's terms and from a mostly personal, non-academic perspective, although I have included thoughts from academicians to support topics and ideas in the book. I also wanted to construct a guide or start a dialogue for those who are finding difficulty in remaining hopeful about the future of kindness in an increasingly angry, and sometimes hostile, world. And, surprisingly, I have found that some people really do not understand kind or nice people, or what motivates those who are sincere or their personal values, so a book was needed. I did not set out to write a book that was difficult to comprehend, where the reader could separate from the ideas I attempted to convey. Nor did I want to create anything as lengthy as Rand's *Atlas Shrugged* or Tolstoy's *War and Peace*; however, like these novels, I wanted to produce and share thought-provoking concepts, but in just slightly under two hundred pages. My personal preference was to also not regurgitate the same information for the sake of "lengthening" the book and, hopefully, this was achieved.

Secondly, it occurred to me that although some people, after meeting me, would refer to me as being "nice." Over the years, and through a lot of interaction and thought, I have found that I am both nice and kind, and there is nothing wrong with being nice, and no stigma intended here. Kind and nice are two words that are used interchangeably. I previously thought that "nice" meant passive and fake, whereas "kind" was more proactive and sincere. To differentiate what I believed was kind from what is considered nice, I constructed a chart, which will appear later in the book to offer a visual and conceptual overview. Kind and nice sincere people are motivated by the well-being of the person for whom the act was intended, without any form of reciprocity expected. What I also found was that being kind meant being sincere, or true to yourself and others, and it is imperative to have the courage to be truly kind. Kindness is often misconstrued in that some people will try to take advantage of your kindness and may consider you to be weak, a doormat, or a pushover. Others, however, would consider you to be attractive, not in the sense of beauty, although there is beauty in being kind, but because your demeanor is open, non-threatening, and supportive, people will seek you out to learn from, not abuse for their personal gain.

People are drawn to those who have a relaxed and welcoming disposition and find people like them to be a beacon in a seemingly uncaring and unsympathetic world. Yes, the sincerely kind and nice are the warriors of the world, and through their courage, generosity, and caring spirit, help others connect with their own kindness center and with this become empowered to positively impact the lives they encounter, exponentially, as in a chain reaction.

CHAPTER 1
WHAT IS COURAGE?

C ourage is the ability to control your fear in a dangerous or difficult situation. It is also the ability to do something that you know is difficult or dangerous—the mental or moral strength to venture, persevere, and withstand danger, fear, or difficulty. In my opinion, courage is not something that a person is born with; rather, it is something that is learned and practiced—and it has everything to do with overcoming fear, if only for the moment. Nelson Mandela beautifully articulated this thinking by saying it is not that we are unafraid, but having courage will conquer that fear. The level of intensity or circumstance can escalate that fear.

This is where the decision is made whether to intervene or determine your next action or inaction. When many people think of courage, they synonymously associate it with danger. Courage, however, can manifest in overcoming a phobia or acting on something that is outside your comfort zone like facing an illness.

Our fears may paralyze us or motivate us into action. The latter is the essence of courage: managing or conquering fear for the moment to propel us into action. The very root word or etymology of courage is "cor"—which is Latin for "heart." It was long believed by past civilizations that feelings of love, empathy, kindness, and other emotions were centered within or derived from the heart. So, if you look at the "cor" of a person, it is not a stretch to feel the need to help others and to show kindness and love during their time of need. The fact that courage has some of its origins in the word "heart" means that we are using our hearts (and minds) to overcome fear and care for or help others.

CHAPTER 2
WHAT IS KINDNESS?

Kindness is the quality of being generous, helpful, and caring about other people, or an act of showing this quality. It is the quality or state of being kind or committing a kind act. In this definition, the word "quality" is often repeated; for kindness is a virtue, and virtues are qualities that humans are capable of exhibiting. The jury is still out as to whether a person can be born kind if they have certain genetic sequences. I believe, however, that a person is not born kind, although one may possess a greater affinity for kindness. Therefore, like courage, kindness must be learned and practiced; it can be random or deliberate, but always purposeful. Its outcome is to benefit the recipient of the kind act and to be selfless in the performance of this action. It is not about you, unlike the way some people view an action or outcome—i.e., "If I do something nice or kind for someone, they will show me the same someday or at some given future time." Latin has a phrase for this: "Quid pro quo"—I do something for you, you do something for me. I consider kindness as being one of the highest of all virtues because when you are kind, you open yourself up to vulnerability. You are focused on that person, not on yourself, and sometimes not even on your own safety. Kindness is like the "breath of God" in that it allows both the giver and recipient a chance to inhale unconditional love and unrelenting compassion, if only for the moment.

CHAPTER 3
WHY HAVING BOTH COURAGE AND KINDNESS IS ESSENTIAL FOR CHANGE

You only need to look at the definitions of courage and kindness to see that these are kindred virtues. There is a symbiotic relationship between these two words, and if practiced, believed, and prayed for, then almost any of us can manifest these virtues. Courageous people without kindness would perhaps be thought of as selfish or reckless in some of their actions. Kind people without courage cannot affect change or empower others. The optimal marriage of these two in a person will elevate the effectiveness of that person's actions and could bring about lasting change.

Is it easy to possess both traits? No, because they both need to be practiced so that, through repetition, one's very minute corpuscles are triggered to respond to or move into courage/kindness mode. You cannot equate this with riding a bicycle—where once you learn how to do it, you will never forget it—even after years of inactive riding. The reason is that each situation that summons you to be both courageous and kind will most likely be unique to that moment. And because they may be different, your approach and application will vary. When you ride a bicycle, you get on and off the same way unless you fall. Even when you try your best in using these virtues, you may not appear outwardly successful. Do not beat yourself up if you think that you failed; at least you tried. Human nature, being as it is, is unpredictable, in that sometimes when you think you have succeeded in helping someone, the result may show failure, and conversely so.

Use the concepts in this book to stimulate your thoughts, your experiences, and that wellspring of hope that lies latent or active within each of us to ease suffering and bring about a better world.

CHAPTER 4

PERSONAL STRUGGLES WITH KINDNESS

Every day when I wake up, I remind myself through positive reinforcement, quiet meditation, or "stillness," that I will not let the events of the day dictate, limit, or diminish my kind attitude or outlook. If you live in or near a big city, like I do, or even if you do not, driving to work, dropping off the kids, going to the store, running errands, seeing a neighbor, sitting on the bus or train, or waiting for an Uber—or whatever—you will likely encounter someone or something that may challenge your optimistic temperament. In other words, you may respond negatively to a situation if you allow it to affect you. I believe it is human nature and an intrinsic part of our DNA as humans that we will more likely than not react in some manner to our surroundings—accept and adapt or challenge and change. However, after this initial encounter, it is up to us to determine how we will embrace or reject that which our five senses and intuition tell us.

I have been told that I am naturally kind and that I have a strong bearing of morality. I believe many of us have these traits and qualities within, and that I am not special, only human, and fallible. I get upset when someone cuts me off while driving, or

I see someone showing disrespect toward or hurting another, especially children or the elderly. And, as you will find later in this book, I still struggle with some of the spiritual concepts of kindness, especially as it relates to those who, in the past, I have considered enemies or adversaries. I must constantly keep things in perspective or run afoul of my morning kindness mantra. Some days are more challenging than others—especially if I am tired or overworked. Unless you practice kindness, live kindness, and remember kindness, you will forget kindness. The courage to be kind is all of this; it is not solely about your condition; it is also about the condition of your fellow man and woman and keeping a balanced and positive outlook.

CHAPTER 5
WHEN KINDNESS ISN'T "STUFF"

It has been said, "If you teach a man to fish and you feed him for a lifetime." How about: If you can show one person what it is like to be kind in her lifetime, she may in turn teach others. Like so many people, I once erroneously thought that you had to give something material or do something physical to show kindness. Many of us were touched a while ago by an act of kindness shown in New York City by one of its police officers. The officer, passing by, noticed an elderly homeless man in the freezing cold with no shoes or socks. The officer asked the man where they were, and he replied that he had none.

The officer proceeded to go into a nearby shoe store and, with his own money, purchased a sturdy pair of shoes for this man. A tourist in the area said she thought about offering the man some money just before the officer showed up. The tourist took a picture of the officer helping the man put on his new shoes, posted it online, and within hours it had gone viral. While this is a very touching story, and the officer is to be applauded for his act of generosity and kindness, we think giving money or purchasing something is the only way to show kindness.

How many times have you walked by someone in need and because you had no money or anything tangible to give, you ignored that person? We do it all the time! We think if we make eye contact with the person, we are then obligated to give or do something monetarily. So, we act as if they do not exist, or pretend not to see them. How about giving them a friendly or comforting smile? Or saying something kind.

Kindness is given without pretense; it is not measured by its sum. One act of kindness could be the key to someone turning their lives around or momentarily easing their current condition or mindset. If you have only material things to give people, then you are not exercising the full range of kindness. There are subliminal things that we can do to show kindness, which is far greater than anything material we could ever give.

Kindness is selfless, as is altruism. Kahlil Gibran says we are to "give" of ourselves and not "stuff" if we are truly helping others. Think about all that you do in your daily routine: You go to work to make money in return to provide for yourself or your family, or to invest in or purchase something. You try to stay in the good graces of your employer so that you might hold onto your position; you expect that if you do a good job, your employer will keep you around. Advertisers on television and the internet tell you that if you are "good" to your spouse or significant other, you will be rewarded with some form of affection or favor.

You help your neighbor out with his leaves, and you might expect him to help you with shoveling your snow, and so on. In each of these scenarios, the implication is that the execution of an act will elicit something in return. Some of us have confused this "expectation" of getting something in return with kindness. However, kindness says—no expectation, no self. You are showing kindness because you first have the means to help (and again, it does not have to be monetary), and secondly, there is someone's need you can fulfill. To be kind is not so much to deny yourself but to share yourself. Let me explain: If you do not care for yourself, you cannot help anyone else, and I do not mean this in a narcissistic manner. If you want to guide others to find their own self-value or self-worth, you cannot do this if you lack these same qualities in who you are or what you perceive yourself to be. There may be times when you will need to tell someone you love that they are on the wrong path, or that you are not going to enable them anymore, and you cannot do this without confidence in who you are. The Ancient Greek maxim, "Know thyself," or self-awareness, is one of the first criteria toward being kind because this gives you the courage to act. If you are unsure of yourself, you cannot share or give the positive affirmations necessary to change lives. You are instead being passively nice, thus, phony because you don't want to offend, or just going along being favorable or agreeable—not kind.

We must be enlightened to be kind, and we must have a higher degree of moral consciousness to show compassion; otherwise, we act from the self or by our own means to an end. It is a tragedy when people think the worst of someone before they have a chance to get to know them. This is called prejudice. We all carry prejudice to some extent within ourselves. We see the person begging and we think of him as a bum, not knowing that he may suffer from mental illness. We see a mother whose kids are wearing tattered clothing, and we label her unfit, even though the clothes may be clean, and she loves her children unconditionally, as with any parent.

What about the person of a different race where we assign stereotypes or instill fear? We also live in a society where if you have "stuff", especially what is considered "nice stuff" (i.e., money, fine houses and cars, fancy clothing, etc.), then you are successful or "okay." As a species, we can be very superficial, and this form of thinking has become more of the norm because we see the way that people with "stuff" are treated. They are usually given instant respect, a coveted place in a restaurant, and even in our religious institutions, people kowtow to them, and these people come to expect this treatment not because of what is in their hearts but rather for the clothes on their backs or the cash in their wallets. An important lesson: You cannot become courageous if you hide behind things. You cannot show kindness if you are also showing prejudice. Even pity can be a form of prejudice because people do not want you to feel sorry for them; they want direction and encouragement. Kindness has the power to show people the courage necessary to overcome their current condition. Kindness extends a hand to lift; pity robs the person of self-worth and subjects them to continuing the same downward trajectory.

After graduating from college, like many young people, I eventually moved out—of—state. Initially, I had landed a job in my hometown with a major national television news network, occasionally writing stories and helping to assemble the news format. I was not fulfilled and had a terrible case of Wanderlust. After spending time in college, then being bound to a stressful job for nearly three years, I wanted to explore and see the world. I saved up some money and briefly thought about getting a newer car, but then decided against it because it would take too much of my stored away "traveling" money. So, I quit my job, packed up my jalopy or what is now referred to as a "hooptie," and headed west, landing in Denver. After a short stint there, I headed to Atlanta, where I had family and initially stayed with my cousins in their apartment.

My hooptie had traveled from the Midwestern US to Denver, and through its harsh winter, then on to Atlanta. By the time "we" arrived in Georgia, we were both tired and beaten down. I was not working initially and did not want to spend the last of the little "traveling" money I had left on another car after living several months in Denver, so cash was at a premium. One cold and unusually snowy Georgia night on the outskirts of the city, my car broke down on the freeway. I was on my way back to my cousins' apartment but was still at least ten miles away. Feeling like this was the start of a streak of bad luck because I did not have much money, so I got out and started walking. There were no cell phones in those days; I was far outside the lighted city, and it was pitch black, besides the tatters of white snow that fell rapidly and threatened to accumulate.

After walking along the freeway for about two miles, a pickup truck pulled up beside me. There sat an elderly man behind the wheel, and I could barely make out anything else about him in the darkness. He reached over to the passenger side of his truck, manually rolled the window down and said, "You want a ride?" This was the early 1980s, during the time of the Atlanta child murders, so initially, I was reluctant to accept his offer. "What if he had a gun?" "What if he were a serial killer?" You may know what I am saying here, but I was so cold and tired somehow that it really did not matter—I just longed for the warmth of the apartment and getting out of the drifting snow. I opened the door and slowly slid into the passenger seat.

The older man asked me where I was heading, and I told him that I did not want to take him too far out of his way and that he could drop me off at the exit leading to my cousins' apartment— which was eight miles from that point. He kindly said, "No," and that he would take me all the way to their place. I thanked him profusely, and when we arrived at the apartment, I offered him all the money that I had on me at the time, which was about ten dollars. He politely refused, to which I then offered to invite him in to take a break and have some coffee to warm up before traveling on. The outline of his face smiled through the darkness, and he said something in his slow and soothing Southern accent that I will never forget. He told me to "Pass the favor along." The elderly gentleman firmly shook my hand, turned his truck around, pulling away with its red taillights melting into the dark of night. If you were to ask me what either he or his truck looked like, to this day, I could not tell you, but his kindness and courage continue to inspire me. When he picked me up, he may have had similar reservations as I did: "Am I picking up a murderer?" "He's a big guy, and I am old; will he do me harm; should I give him a lift?" Or did he reason that in having passed my car broken down by the side of the highway and it being very cold that I could have used his help.

I know that God will sometimes send his angels to intervene in our lives and help us out, and this man showing up when he did was both a miracle and a blessing. We must believe in the goodness of the human spirit and ask God to protect and guide us as we pass His kindness on to others. We should also find the courage to overcome our fears, such as this man did, because we may never know the full impact of how much one act of kindness can have over a lifetime. Whoever he was and wherever he is, he helped change my life. I am truly humbled, grateful, thankful, and encouraging everyone to "pass the favor along."

CHAPTER 6
WHY SOME FEAR BEING KIND

In the United States, we are defined by our toughness. We idolize the person who takes matters into their own hands and walks away a winner. This same person rarely shows emotion and is even less portrayed as being kind. Why? Because any inkling of kindness would destroy the image that we hold in our minds about people like them—you cannot be bold or tough and caring or sympathetic. At one time, this attitude carried over into the corporate world in that bosses who were smart but perceived as being "emotionally connected" or had emotional intelligence, or now referred to as EQ, did not last too long or would be typecast as a weak or ineffectual leader. Daniel Goleman's blockbuster book, *Emotional Intelligence: Why It Can Matter More Than IQ*, dispelled this myth. He pointed out that success is not entirely dependent on IQ, but having emotional intelligence—altruism, empathy, love, and mindfulness—is more important. Still, some believe it is the perceived gladiator, the one who enters the arena absent of emotion or empathy, with a will to 'win at all costs' mindset, as being the ideal prototype of a strong leader. This person has very little time to take someone's weakness and help develop it into a strength, with the outcome favorable to the good of both the individual and group. You either come prepared for war or you die. This is one of the many reasons we fear being kind—the stigma of weakness. If you are weak, you can become a "mark" for unscrupulous people or a victim of your own kindness. In a warped example of someone taking advantage of the kindness of others, Ted Bundy serves as a poster child. As a ploy to lure young women into his web of debauchery, he would feign a handicap or wear crutches to pretend to be incapable of performing a physical act. As soon as the innocent woman would come to his aid (i.e., show kindness or concern), he would strike her with something—tire iron, etc.—knocking her unconscious, then murder her. So, we wear the façade of being tough as though it were a weakness repellant and not taking anything off anybody.

Road rage fits into this weakness category. You cut in front of me, or you make a maneuver as we are driving down the road and now, I am mad. You insulted my psyche and made me look like a loser, and now I need to "one-up" you by doing everything possible to get in front of you. Civility is now null, and it is all-out war with escalation and whipping in and out of traffic until one of you comes to your senses and breaks off this madness or you kill yourselves or some other innocent soul. When we are kind, we show a rare side of our psyche that throws all animalistic evolutionary survival tactics out the window. We are genuinely interested in the well-being of fellow humans, alleviating their suffering through acts of selflessness, not survival of the fittest. There is little fear; only courage and kindness toward someone in need. It also takes wisdom and selflessness to not retaliate as in the road rage example. If we are egoic in our thinking, we personalize every action that we perceive as negative as a threat to this ego. So, to appease the ego, we strike back at the "perpetrator" and try to take back the piece of the ego that was lost through their alleged actions.

Joseph Carey Merrick was born in 1862 in London, England, and was seriously deformed. To earn his stay in his home, he was forced out onto the streets to sell goods. Due to his appearance, he was brutally teased and upon seeing his face, people literally went into shock. He eventually struck out on his own landing in a London workhouse. The workhouses were where poor people could find shelter and food in exchange for work and were notorious for inflicting extreme cruelty and abuse on its residents. From there, he went on to become a circus oddity and was shown kindness but only a few times in his short life—most significantly by Dr. Frederick Treves, a surgeon, who provided Joseph with his first and last permanent home in Whitechapel Hospital. Despite all the taunting and hurt that Joseph encountered, it is said that he was caring, gentle, and kind.

The Elephant Man, as he was called, should have been the very first person to fear being kind to others, and for good reason! Why should he be kind toward an unkind world that had labeled him a "freak," or worse, an animal? He should have been bitter and afraid of people after all that he had endured, yet he was just the opposite. He showed the world that there were many physically attractive people who were unkind and ugly inside and that one should never judge based solely on appearance. He had a "hideous" outward appearance, which cloaked a beautiful soul. We can take courage from Joseph Carey Merrick because he was never afraid to show kindness—whether to the man in the street or the royalty of England who came to visit him at the hospital where he resided.

Then, there is the person receiving the act of kindness being suspicious of or fearing the person showing kindness. They wonder, "Why are they being so nice to me—and they don't even know me?" Or "What do they want from me now that they have shown kindness toward me?" There are also people who want to show kindness who ask themselves— "Will this person rob me if I give them money or curse at me should I offer nothing but a kind word?" This is where courage comes in and fear leaves. To make a difference through kindness requires doing something in the face of fear or mistrust but with discernment. Later in the book, I devote a chapter to discernment and kindness as necessities.

I remember some years ago when I worked at Mayo Clinic in Rochester, Minnesota, I had recently had my Achilles tendon surgically repaired following a sports-related injury. It was a very cold winter evening as I was preparing to leave for home, and not far from my office building, I saw a guy standing on the sidewalk begging for money. And even though I was on crutches, I stopped and reached for my pocket to give him money. As I was handing him the money, he reached with both hands for my hand acting as though he were eagerly thanking me, but I noticed that he was trying to slide the gold college ring from my finger. This man had surmised that if he made off with my ring, there would be no way for me to physically chase him down and retrieve it. So, I pulled my hand back and looked squarely at him and he realized I knew he was trying to take my ring. He had a strange look afterwards. Maybe he thought about what he had tried to do. Perhaps he was now afraid of what I might do to him even though I was semi-incapacitated. I just looked sternly at him, without saying a word, then turned and hobbled away. I felt violated and betrayed. I had also interjected "self" into the situation because it hurt me and momentarily shook my confidence in helping strangers. How could this seemingly down-on-his-luck man attempt to steal my ring after I had stopped to give him money on this brutally cold Minnesota evening?

I was reminded of the parable of the Good Samaritan, as told by Jesus— "A certain man went down from Jerusalem to Jericho, and fell among thieves, which stripped him of his raiment, and wounded him, and departed, leaving him half dead. And by chance there came down a certain priest that way; and when he saw him, he passed on the other side. And likewise, a Levite, when he was at the place, came and looked in on him, and passed by on the other side. But a certain Samaritan, as he journeyed, came where he was: and when he saw him, he had compassion on him, and went to him, and bound up his wounds, pouring in oil and wine, and set him on his own beast, and brought him to an inn, and took care of him. And on the morrow when he departed, he took out two pence, and gave them to the host, and said unto him, Take care of him; and when I come again, I will repay thee."

Remember, the Samaritans were the sworn enemy of the Jews—which the injured man was. We must be as the Samaritan; despite what we think of the person, regardless of their race, ethnicity, gender, sexual orientation, political beliefs, or religion, or how the recipient of our kindness reacts or reciprocates, this person may need our help. Through our kindness, we can transform people. I have often thought—Is this guy still out robbing others or pretending to be in need only to lay traps for people? Or did my reaction give this man pause to transform himself from thief to belief? The Bible teaches, "Let him that stole steal no more: but rather let him labour, working with his hands the thing which is good, that he may have to give to him that needeth."

Some people think of kind people as being pushovers; that if you do something kind for someone, you may then become their "mark" or are a fool. There are a lot of people who would be kind or could be kind but are afraid of letting their guard down and getting typecast as being weak. This is fear, and it takes courage to show kindness, especially to a stranger—whether opening the door for them, helping with their cart in a store, reaching for or retrieving something for someone who is in a wheelchair, giving money or offering a kind word to someone on a street corner. The other day, while shopping at a grocery store, I turned a corner and down the aisle saw a man jumping up and down trying to reach for something high on a shelf. After several unsuccessful attempts, I asked if I could help—to which he agreed—then said, "Grab as many of those as you can, please!" So, being over six feet tall and feeling his embarrassment after he resorted to literally cursing himself for being short in stature, I handed him several of the items. I then quickly intervened and told him not to worry or berate himself, and I was there to help him. I shook his hand and said, "God bless you!" and walked away. There are times when we will know or discern whether to intervene and help or not. This was one of those times when a kind act was needed and appreciated.

Sometimes our fear is rooted in not wanting to get shot down, embarrassed, or harassed— "No one asked you to open the door for me!" Or "Come on, is that all you're going to give me?" Or "If I need your help, I'll ask you!" And, if you are truly kind, you give or intervene because you care about that person, you do not worry about how they will react to your kindness, you do it because someone has asked for help or has shown need, like the man in the store. Another reality is that some people do not want or need your help when offered. To this point, here is something extreme an anonymous person posted that I found while surfing the web:

"Driving through somewhat rural parts surprisingly near Silicon Valley, I once passed an abandoned SUV that had been pulled over and parked somewhat inappropriately—there was not enough room on the side of the road, so the vehicle was sticking out into the lane a little. A half-mile further, I saw a businesswoman in an expensive suit, with her bag and purse, walking down the road. She had clearly run out of gas. I pulled over to the side, rolled down my window, and said, 'Looks like you could use a little help...' Before I could finish, with 'because the nearest gas station is about five miles away,' she had already spit right in my face and eyes, through the window. You can be 100% sure someone needs your help. You can never be sure if they will accept it."

Do you think this person will offer to help the next person who they see whose car has broken down on the highway? Their fear may be justified in this case, and they were "shot down" in their attempt at kindness, but they must not give in to it forever. The lady could have been on her way to an important interview, planning to meet with a key client, or any number of circumstances when she allegedly ran out of gas. Perhaps, she thought the person trying to help her was being sarcastic or trying to make light of her situation depending on the tone delivered, and she was clearly not in the mood. We may never know, but do not give up—have the courage to try, try, again.

Another important point is kindness does not always mean that you give for the sake of giving; there are times you will need to have the courage to say "no" to something, as well. Or even speak up when you see where this person may be misdirected through your act of kindness. For instance, if you see where your kindness can lead to someone's destruction, alcohol, or drug use, for example, or if someone is heading down the wrong path and you say nothing and stand idly by, or you enable or aid them in their self-destruction, then that is neither an act of courage nor kindness. Because you are or should be interested in the well-being of the person, you will be compelled to speak out and show that person where they are wrong. Not that you are judging them, but you should have some degree of insight as to whether your act will lead the person to continue down a certain road or to change direction and minimize or prohibit their self-destructiveness.

It takes a lot of courage to be kind. We look at the television and we see someone who is supposedly showing strength and courage by putting someone down or berating them, but that is showing neither. A lot of this behavior is fear-based because that person wants to inflict pain on someone else before any pain can be brought down on them. So, they will lash out to try and minimize or neutralize the other person to render them ineffective—"Do unto others, before they do unto you!" How often have you seen this in your own lives? There are those who relish this type of behavior because they think they are operating from a point of strength, especially when they have an audience. It is more important to them to show their "superiority" over others. They feel as if they act this way, they will gain the respect of others or observers—through fear or outright intimidation. To have courage is to overcome fear; to be kind is to overcome what others think of you because what others think of you is not important. What is most important is doing what is right. Many people are surprised when kindness is shown to them because it can be so unexpected nowadays, and sometimes uncommon. If we quit trying to dominate one another, perhaps we will learn how to love, and through this love, we will create a better world. This applies to both individuals and nations.

I had another experience where my courage and kindness were both tested. I was on the East Coast (United States) attending a conference in a large city and had a room at one of its hotels. One beautiful sun-strewn morning, as I headed toward the building where my conference was being held, I could not overlook the beautiful avenue covered with boutiques and other specialty shops. There were people out and I saw a woman approaching; the first person whose path I crossed shortly after leaving the hotel. Being from the Midwest it is almost habitual that we speak to or acknowledge others, even strangers. She looked at me until we were within thirty yards, then she dropped her head and looked down toward the ground. As we passed one another, I said, "Good morning," and she never looked up or said anything; just kept on walking.

Since it was my first time in this city, I surmised that here you do not talk to strangers, and I knew I was no longer in the Midwest. I walked about a half block and saw a man approaching, so I dropped my head and walked by him, again thinking that this was the norm. To my astonishment, I heard, "Hello!" It was not a "half hello," but a full, heartfelt, and kindly greeting. I returned the salutation, feeling somewhat rude, if not embarrassed. I took a few more paces then turned around and called out to him. He stopped, turned around, and waited. I walked over to him and shared my encounter with the woman and that I was a stranger in town. He proceeded to lay down the rules. "First," he said with emphasis, "I always make it a point to greet people because I'm from here and I want everyone to feel welcomed. Secondly, you never approach anyone and speak to them directly; they fear that you might be trying to run a scam on them, rob, or take advantage of them." He continued, "Now, if the person has a dog, you could ask to pet the dog, then ask about the breed, and only then you can start to converse with them. Or, if they have small children, you can remark how beautiful their children are, then start a more in-depth conversation. People here are very suspicious, but I personally want to wish you a warm welcome to our city and hope you will come back to visit us again!"

What a difference one person's kindness made! Now in defense of the lady, maybe she acted that way because she had neither a dog, nor child, and I am not exactly a small person. So, perhaps, that is why she did not speak. I will never know. But I do know that one person's kindness can make a difference in someone's life—if they have the courage to show it. Surely, there were people who would not speak to him either. But that did not concern him—he was going to be friendly and show kindness and welcoming warmth regardless. I found strength and learned an important lesson through his actions—Be fearless!

What is kindness without courage as I asked earlier in the book? It is like having the capacity to change but not the will or courage to change. To achieve anything great in life takes courage and preparation. If you want to take on a challenge, though you lack the courage and readiness to meet it head on, you will not achieve greatness. Here, I do not equate greatness with fortune, fame, or some other fleeting human value, but rather the desire to accomplish something; something that you set out to do and you do—with all your sinew and will. Kindness is like that; we can get sidetracked by the negative things and people we encounter, or we can overcome these influences by deploying our continuation to be kind through courage.

When your kindness is rebuffed, exploited, questioned, etc., keep being kind—do not give up! You will never know the difference you can make in someone's life—if you do not try or become indifferent or apathetic. You just may change the very person who turned away your kindness. They may begin to think about how you tried to help them, and this may be the very spark that is needed to send them on their own personal journey toward kindness and self-awareness. This stranger's kindness has inspired me to someday visit that city again and with a whole new outlook.

In the early stages of writing this book, I shared with my sister its general concept and she was able to relate to many of the conditions and situations that I was preparing to write about. What moved me most during our conversation was when she reminded me of our own late mother and how she showed kindness to others, even though some were not as kind to her in return. We talked about why our mother did not waver from being kind to people. It was "not as if they were using me," mother would always say, but rather, she knew her reward was not to be found in this world and that God would acknowledge her kindness, which was more important. As youths, we would sometimes scratch our heads, wondering why she continued to be kind to certain people. This rubbed off on me and my siblings, for we are kind people, and despite the actions of others, like our mother, we continue to show kindness to those who think they may be using us. We have learned the courage to be kind by example.

If we can only show others the strength and peace there is to be gained by not getting bogged down by external conjecture or internalized feelings of being used and plow forward, knowing that the true spirit of kindness comes from a source far greater than ourselves.

CHAPTER 7

WHEN OTHERS USE OR ABUSE YOUR KINDNESS

This complements why some would fear being kind, and it deserves its own chapter. Like many of you, I have experienced people trying to take advantage of my kindness, and through discernment, prayer, and over time, I learned how to quickly surmise when a relationship is too one-sided. This is where you are the giver of kindness, and the other is the taker. As I discussed earlier, in kindness you should expect nothing in return, but this does not equate to being used, abused, or "run over." We should continue to be kind, but not a doormat where, for the sake of kindness and peace and altruism, we turn a blind eye to the "user."

I had an acquaintance some years back who only called me when he needed something or wanted me to do him a favor; otherwise, I would never hear from him. Over time, it became clear that he was a user, that he had nothing to contribute to the relationship but wanted the benefit of having another source that could fulfill his needs. After much thought and prayer, I made a conscious decision to not let this person use me or my kind and helpful ways anymore. So, I slowly distanced myself from him and, in doing so, freed up energy and time to help others who were sincere in needing my help.

Then there are those who will try and take your kindness from you, sometimes by putting you down: "He's a phony, no one can be that positive all the time!" or "I don't like her because she seems 'so happy' every time I see her." Sincerely kind and nice people are upbeat about life, not beat down by it, so they project an air of hope and positivity, and it is not illusionary or Pollyannaish—it is real! So, for those who do not understand kind people, they may peg them as not living realistically or trapped in a "fool's paradise"—absent of doom and gloom. Kind and nice sincere people know that doom and gloom exist, but they choose to not let it affect their inner joy or outer confidence; whatever may happen. Greater is that spirit of hope that dwells within them than the doubt found within the world, and they believe in possibilities.

The realities of ugliness and shallowness exist, but kind and nice sincere people see themselves as making a difference from, not a contribution to, the negativity in the world. Therefore, do not let anyone abuse or take your kindness—it is special and is intended to uplift hearts and empower—not used as a tool for egoism. Take the example of the hawk. Although it is a bird of prey, it is easily attacked by other birds should it fly too low. So, use your "kindness" wings to soar higher in altitude and attitude.

CHAPTER 8
"GOODY-TWO SHOES," WHY ARE YOU SUCH A THREAT TO SOME?

Kind and nice, sincere people have been 'labeled' since time immemorial; many of these given names are very unflattering. In some chapters, I discuss where there is a tendency for kind or nice, sincere people to be misunderstood or thought of as being insincere. Also, why some feared being known as either. Not judging here, but some people are prone to misbehaving and look for ways to get into things they know are not right. So, if you are a kind and nice, sincere person, who do you think they want to hang around with? Right, not you! The reason being is because kind and nice, sincere people value and practice doing what is right, and a person like that tagging along will remind the person doing or wanting to do wrong why he or she should not do so. Therefore, you might not get invited to hang out at "certain parties," and some people will avoid you altogether.

I remember while growing up that my mother did not drink or smoke or play cards, and there is nothing wrong with this if done in moderation (for the sake of your health), and I am not here to judge anyone. She was also in church about two to three times a week. From what I can recall, mother was never invited to some of the trendy parties around the community and city. Now, to justify why she may not have been asked to attend certain functions, perhaps, people knew she did not do many of the things they did, and in excess, including being unfaithful to their husbands and wives. They considered her "unhip" or "behind the times," and despite all of this, mother had her family and many friends. She was content with being "the square," as she said she was sometimes called.

When you are kind or nice and sincere, expect not to be invited to some parties, or where people are planning to do wrong things, because the way in which you carry yourself may serve as a threat to consciousness. No one likes to be reminded of behaving badly, and your very presence communicates this loud and clear. Do not internalize this "cold shoulder" or change to fit in; continue to practice kindness and doing the right thing. It takes courage to stand out from the crowd and not just go along, and it is far easier to get into trouble than to get out of it. Find people who also do not follow an immoral or amoral path in life but are comfortable and confident with who they are as kind and nice, sincere people, and equally important, with who you are.

More people will be interested in hanging out with you when you are kind or nice and sincere, than if you are a mischief-maker. Kind and nice, sincere people are attractive to non-misbehaving types because they feel they can relax and be themselves rather than always being on the defense to fit in or win approval. To people like this, you are not a threat; you are a companion and confidant, and you will always feel genuinely welcomed at their parties, homes, and events.

CHAPTER 9
KIND OR NICE? DON'T LET OTHERS CHANGE YOU!

The following are excerpts that were pulled from the internet nearly verbatim. I did not include any identifiers of the authors to help maintain their anonymity:

Person 1:
"I remember back in school when I was a nice guy. nothing gave me more pleasure than putting a smile on another face in any way I could. But I began to notice that people looked down on me for it! So I worked real hard to go against my natural desire to be nice and became an *******. It took a lot of techniques and willpower and repetition, but I finally became a big *** and now people respect me, and I have everything I wanted in life…still, it's very confusing, why didn't they just look up to me for being a nice guy for all my acts of kindness. Every day now, I think of so many awesome things I could do to help people as a well-funded, intelligent, and able-bodied adult but I never do any of it cause I know I'll just be looked down at as being a big loser people pleaser. It seems to be common in society to respect and honor those who are tuff, ruthless, and take what they want, and look down on those who are kind, obedient,

and helpful. I guess nobody wants a world where everyone is trying to help one another?? Why is society like that??"

Person 2:
"Hey guys, You see I am a person that tries to do the best I can and trying to live my life right, but it seems like I get hated for no reason for being the 'white knight,' so to speak. So, I ask you guys, why do people hate the kind, nice stand-up guy? I am a person that doesn't drink, doesn't smoke, doesn't hang out in clubs, and works hard for what I do, but yet I get criticized for being that way. I try to love others no matter what, but some people make it difficult. What makes this wrong? Is it because I am different from the world? I don't understand it at all. I don't plan to change, but I am just wondering why do people do this. I have been called 'fake,' 'not sincere,' and everything under the blue moon. Thank you for your help in advance."

These personal stories could easily fall under the chapter of "Why Some People Fear Being Kind," however, it needed its own because it is a reality faced by tens of thousands, if not millions, of kind and sincere people throughout the world. The pressure of conforming or "fitting in," along with the fear of being disrespected, drives some kind people to change. Everyone, to some degree, wants to be accepted somewhere or by someone, so when there is rejection or accusations of falsehood, our first instinct is to self-assess, and most times negatively. We begin to internalize the bad karma being heaped on us and, because of our egos, we need to push out this negativity or counter it by feeding this ego the antithesis of what we believe. We then start to adopt those beliefs and behaviors that we think will help us to fit in, feel appreciated, or respected.

In the two examples, the first person essentially forced himself to change from being a nice person into a "jerk." He surmised that when you are nice, or kind, you open yourself up to all forms of rejection and disrespect. By repetitively "practicing" being a jerk, and being perceived by others as one, he describes the outcome as being liberating because he now has all the respect and outward trappings of success, which he feels he could not have achieved by being a kind person or nice guy. He has essentially embraced the "nice guys finish last" line of reasoning. What is most interesting here is that he is a "closet" kind and nice sincere person who continues to wrestle with why he could not be more accepted for his kindness and questions why "nobody wants a world" where people help one another. There are also slight hints that he is miserable trying to be something he is not. He is not a jerk, but rather a nice and kind sincere person living in the illusion of one.

In the second example, the person talks about "being hated for no reason" and questions why this happens when he tries to "love others, no matter what." This may be a case of a person who is subconsciously displaying phony kind traits in that he states that he "does not drink, or smoke or hang out in clubs, and works hard" and perceives himself as being that of a "white knight" or rescuer of those in distress. Well, as I stated before, it is not about you externally, or your image or what others think about you, it is about what is in your heart and the purpose behind what you do. And, while it appears that his heart may be in the right place, is he helping people or playing the white knight for self-serving reasons? If you want to be perceived as a kind person, as in this example—then you are trying too hard and, thus, not being entirely true to yourself or others.

Kind and nice sincere people come from all walks of life—they drink, they smoke, they hang out in clubs, they work hard, and they do some things that many people do, but what differentiates them from others is that they feel a higher sensitivity toward people and their hearts, or "cor," will always tell them to do the right thing. They do not wear kindness on their sleeves—they actively practice it, and most times discreetly. Their purpose is not to enable others or draw attention to their acts of kindness, but upon their quality as selfless human beings. Yes, when you are sincerely kind or nice, you are sometimes "suspect" in that people will call you insincere, or fake, but do not change — re-examine your motives. Are you being kind for your own selfish need to be perceived as such, like the phony kind or nice person, or are you being kind because you really want to help others regardless of what someone thinks of you? It is admirable that this person does not plan to change, but if their self-assessment shows that they are being insincere to themselves, they may need to change—for the better.

So, do not change from being kind just to fit in or satisfy others' opinions of yourself because you never will. Find the strength to resist and change only if you feel the need to modify your current thinking and behavior, and please make it sincere and positive. The courage to be kind when practiced should change you from being reactionary to becoming revolutionary, thus, controlling your emotions and disrupting the status quo through selfless kind acts. Others observing your kindness can, perhaps, learn from this and become transformative in their thinking.

"A chrysalis is but hidden beauty awaiting change."
~ J. Touché

CHAPTER 10
BITTERNESS AS AN ENEMY OF KINDNESS

We all have baggage that we carry along with us throughout life, but the worst of this 'baggage,' in my opinion, manifests itself through bitterness. Bitterness is where you allow the actions of others or situations to deeply affect your mood, thoughts, or behavior—whether short or long-term. In his book, *A New Earth*, Eckhart Tolle describes bitterness as a form of the "pain-body"—where we are scarred from past emotional pain, or baggage, that we have not fully confronted or overcome, and we summon up this pain unconsciously—and people or events can sometimes serve as a "trigger" for its manifestation.

We have all read, seen, or heard about the poignant book, *A Christmas Carol*, by Charles Dickens. In the story, we find the lead character, Ebenezer Scrooge, sent off to a boarding school: a distant father, and a mother who died in childbirth bringing him into the world. He is lonely, and his father blames him for taking the life of his beloved wife, and he is bitter toward him. The impact of his father's dislike of him follows Scrooge throughout most of his life and guides much of his thinking and behavior until he is redeemed by his one-time, now deceased, business partner, Jacob Marley, and the three spirits who follow his appearance. In the end, he is liberated from his "pain-body" and emerges as a thoughtful, kind, and loving person.

Bitterness also keeps us from showing kindness and blinds us to the profound reality of its impact on those around us; it is a mixture of fear, anger, and mistrust. Once you are bitter, you wear these like a cocoon around you. It protects and insulates you and keeps you from getting hurt again. Because of this fear, you distrust the motives of those who try to penetrate your cocoon of bitterness and become angry with anyone who attempts to get too close. You have seen it in others, or you have experienced this bitterness, and while you were wrapped in it, you lacked empathy or concern for anyone other than yourself. How long will you wear the cocoon of bitterness? The oft-repeated story is told of the woman or man who shuns any advances of love or affection or trust because of the deep hurt from a past relationship. They spurn love and closeness because they are afraid of being "let down" again. You may know someone like this, or it may even be yourself. Take the time to think about how this is impacting yourself and others, and how your legacy may end up being unkind due to your lack of courage to identify, confront, and overcome this "pain-body."

CHAPTER 11

ASSERTIVENESS IS ESSENTIAL TO BEING COURAGEOUS AND KIND

Somehow the erroneous message got out that you cannot be both assertive and kind. Many associate kindnesses with meekness. Here, I speak of the biblical meaning of the word "meek," which is to trust in the Lord and his ways, refraining from anger or revenge, and being humble, not arrogant. In this sense, you can be both meek and assertive. It is this assertiveness that pushes action, which neither kindness nor meekness can do alone. If you see someone needing direction, or if change is to occur in the person to whom kindness is being directed, you will need to be truthful with them and show them that they are not being kind to themselves. This is where assertiveness and courage have their greatest impact: the presence to motivate others and change lives. Another common misnomer is that kind people exude or should show passivity. No, the truly kind are confident, not arrogant, in both speech and mannerism because they act from a point of purpose, compassion, and selflessness, so there is no need for being passive or submissive. They also know that effective change cannot happen exclusively through passive measures.

To this point, when we study Mahatma Gandhi and his struggle to liberate India from British rule, his strategy of Satyagraha, or nonviolence, was initially observed by some as being passive only, not passive resistance. It was intended to not destroy the British or drive them from his country using force, but to bring them to the truth and change their hearts and minds. When we are kind, we too are all about truth and changing both hearts and minds. We do this by giving hope and truth to the recipients of our kindness, and perhaps through this spark of compassion and revelation, it may create a fire within that will prevent them from slipping back into their former existence or state of mind. Assertiveness, not passivity, intertwined with purpose, freedom, and independence through courage is that which Gandhi sought and achieved.

CHAPTER 12

WHAT KINDNESS ISN'T
IT'S NOT ALL NICE!

As mentioned in an earlier chapter, kind people are also referred to as "nice." In essence, kind people do kind and nice things, but some kind people will quickly disassociate themselves from exclusively "nice" labels. Why? There is an assumed difference between being kind and being nice. I have developed a chart below to illustrate both similarities and differences, and I want to emphasize here there is nothing wrong with being called nice. Furthermore, and most importantly, there should not be a stigma associated with it. Being sincerely kind and nice means doing something for your fellow human or living thing for his, her, or its benefit. It is from the heart, as one friend of mine explained—the "cor." Whereas, to some people, being kind or nice is simply camouflaging one's actions through self-serving, deceptive means.

Many times, people have said to me, "I'm through with this person or that because after all that I've done for them, they never thanked me." Or "I helped _____ through some hard times they were having and now that they've gotten back on their feet, I don't hear from them!" You know why you feel this way? It is because you went into it consciously or subconsciously with the expectation that if you did a kind act for someone, you would be repaid with kindness—WRONG! That person was there in your life at that moment because you were able to help them when no one else would, could, or was willing to. In the "moment," things line up, then fall into place. There is no prologue or epilogue to kindness; it just happens, then it is gone, and you let go. But, if you entered the kind act with self, instead of selfless ego, then you may feel hurt. What you did was phony kind, or phony nice, not sincerely kind, and nice. Once you understand the differences and similarities between these three areas, the better you will be able to handle the aftermath. Kindness expects nothing in return; it gives for the sake of giving.

The adage that nice guys finish last is neither factual nor applicable to sincerely nice and kind people. It is the phony nice person who is the one that sucks up to everyone or lacks the courage to not let people walk all over him or her. Not judging here, but he or she is a living doormat—no guts. They are afraid of being truthful and if you are going to be sincerely nice and kind, this is a prerequisite. They hide behind a smile that cloaks a broken man or woman. Yes, he or she finishes last because if they were sincerely kind and nice instead of phony nice, they would have defined themselves as being strong (by the words he or she chooses, or the way in which he or she carries themselves) and confident long before it got to the point where they were being used—and perceptive people and potential "users" would have been aware of this.

You can choose either to live triumphantly or tragically, and you must first respect yourself before you can respect anyone else. Think of phony nice people as victims and sincere kind and nice people as victors because to be victorious in any endeavor requires courage. I should point out here, the phony kind person is also a victim in that he or she manufactures kindness to make themselves look good and are therefore victims of their own selfish egos.

The illustrated chart below was created to help differentiate between what I believe is kind and what is nice.

KIND & NICE SINCERE	KIND/PHONY
	NICE/PHONY

This graph shows where many people fall in terms of nice and kind. When I constructed this grid, it was a result of a debate that I was having in that my original perception of niceness was insincerity and passive. The grid helped me to see that it was as possible to be kind and nice and sincere as it was possible to be kind and phony or nice and phony. Sincere people selflessly serve others and are confident and assertive. Phony people are self-serving, or seek to please others, and are insecure or passive.

Kind and Nice Sincere
Being sincerely kind and nice means when you are in this quadrant, you display what I call "active kindness" because if you see someone in need of a kind deed, or intervention, you are there to help and are engaged. People who fall into this area are also not afraid to tell you the truth, even if it hurts, because it is not their intention to bring pain, but to help you avoid greater pain and suffering. They make for great friends in that they are

sincere in their intentions and interactions; especially with people with whom they are close. You always know where they stand, and they tend not to sugarcoat difficult topics or avoid unpleasant situations. They want to help build an all-inclusive society where everyone can benefit. People are attracted to kind and nice sincere types because they appear confident and give off an aura of having self-control and level-headedness. They come in all forms; some outgoing or forceful and others more amiable, soft-spoken, perhaps, quiet, or shy—not passive—and work behind the scenes. They are "wise as serpents and harmless as doves." Do not confuse them with the nice/phony group, or you will be in for a big surprise! They may appear outgoing, quiet, friendly, aloof, or shy, but they know who they are, and they are confident and selfless; one of the touchstones of true kindness and niceness. You will not be able to "walk over" or exploit people in this quadrant.

Kind/Phony

Kind/Phony people appear to be kind, but they are not. They perform kind acts deceptively and mostly to bring attention to themselves, and they will work hard at it. They tend to be very narcissistic and untrustworthy. Having and using discernment will usually allow you to cut through the mask to see their true nature. People in this quadrant are phonies and have no allegiance to anyone but themselves. You probably know, or have met, someone like this. They purposely and consciously know that they are deceiving others and try to manipulate them by pretending to be kind. They are cunning, calculating, and sometimes diabolical, wolves in sheep's clothing. Kind/Phony people will often hide behind their religion or present themselves as "holier-than-thou," or try to appear highly moral and ethical. Do not be snookered in by their smooth words. Watch their actions and behaviors, and this will tell you who they are and what is in their hearts.

Nice/Phony

People in this quadrant are the ones who get "walked on" because they either consciously or subconsciously come across as being "nice," but lack the courage to stand up for themselves or what is right. These people are the descriptive "wimp" and end up getting hurt or used by others because their demeanor and behavior signals— "weak." They become the primary targets of ruthless people like the kind/phony types, because like sharks which smell blood in the water, will flesh out and find nice/phony people to dominate and exploit.

The nice/phony people are not necessarily evil or devious, they are most times just the opposite. They crave acceptance by any means necessary and will often overcompensate for being liked; just going along with whatever or whomever whether right or wrong. They are known to kiss up to people and seek approval and are repulsed by most everyone except kind and nice sincere people. Like the kind/phony, they care more about their image and what others think of them rather than the truth. These people-pleasers end up deceiving themselves and feeling miserable after they have allowed others to mistreat and disrespect them. It is in this quadrant where you will find the proverbial "nice guys finish last" people. If they would stop trying to please everyone and be true to themselves and others, regardless of the consequences, they could possibly move into the kind and nice sincere quadrant.

CHAPTER 13
CAN ANYONE BE KIND? CAN WE CHANGE?
THE CHALLENGE OF REPROGRAMMING OUR KINDNESS

I believe that although we have the capability to be kind or improve upon it, due to environmental influences, fear, past negative experiences, daily survival, or plain apathy, our kindness sometimes gets shoved to the back of our consciousnesses. So, what if kindness does not come easy for you? It should not make you feel as though you are cruel or uncaring; you may need some reprogramming. Your ability to change is only as great as your willingness and commitment to allow change. As humans, we sometimes erect barriers between ourselves and others, and this is mostly due to uncertainty, insecurity, mistrust, or fear. We want to insulate ourselves from any emotional upheavals in our lives, and if you are going to show kindness, you may occasionally be drawn into an emotional situation.

Courage is needed to overcome these barriers because we cannot be effective if we are engulfed in fear. I am not advocating that you put yourself in harm's way, by any means, but to allow that part of you that seeks detachment or wants to run away, embrace the situation, and grow in action to become an agent of change. The work of one of the most influential behavior-change theorists of the 20th century, James O. Prochaska, PhD, had a profound influence on me. In studying his and Carlo C. DiClemente, PhD, *Transtheoretical Model of Behavior Change*, I found it could not only be applicable to improved health outcomes but might also apply to a much wider range of behaviors and motivations, including kindness. I have inserted kindness into this model and developed the chart below:

The Stages of Kindness Change using the Transtheoretical Model developed by Prochaska and DiClemente are identified as:

Pre-contemplation: The person does not consider being kind. The person may have tried previously and unsuccessfully but, due perhaps to past failed attempts toward kindness, the person denies its importance. They feel any act of altruism will not work or change/benefit others.

Contemplation: The person is ambivalent or apathetic about showing kindness. Reaching out to others or changing their view of helping others makes them feel uncomfortable because they are accustomed to letting others make a difference. During this stage, people assess barriers ("I don't have time to volunteer or work one-on-one with someone," "I'm struggling to make ends meet, and I can't afford to spend a dime to help," "I don't want the hassle of having to drive that distance—gas isn't cheap, you know." Or "I'm too afraid to go into that area with all of the crime that's over there.").

Preparation: The person conscientiously decides to try kindness. They may take small steps at showing kindness, such as helping a stranger or helping cut an elderly person's grass, as their determination to change increases.

Action: The person is actively engaged in showing kindness regularly. If the prior stages have been neglected, action itself is often not enough. Reward yourself (e.g., splurging on an ice cream sundae, going to your favorite restaurant, etc.) for showing kindness or helping others because it demonstrates the selfless desire for change.

Maintenance and Relapse Prevention: Relapse prevention is necessary to maintain this new change; minimize negative external influences or internal thoughts that may lead to relapse. The person may need to find and associate with kindred spirits who believe in the importance of kindness and making a difference as a form of support and maintenance.

Termination: The person is self-sufficient in applying kindness in his or her life. Practicing kind deeds may become habitual at this point; however, continued support from those in the maintenance group may be needed to extend and reinforce positive behaviors.

Try using this model, whatever stage you are currently at, to see if you can reprogram, rekindle, or maintain your kindness. I would enjoy hearing whether you experienced a change in your motivation using these steps.

CHAPTER 14

THE FUTURE OF KINDNESS

With the rise of the internet and other social media, there exists the capacity for us to disconnect from others on a more physical and emotional level. What this may indicate is that the more physical and emotional distance we as a species put between ourselves, the greater the capacity for us to lose feeling and closeness to one another. From a communications standpoint, our ability to keep in touch and communicate has never been greater since the beginning of time.

It is instant, far-reaching, informative, and sometimes destructive. If you go onto the internet and enter some blogs or forums, you will see that people are saying things to and about each other that they would never say in person. What this shows is we can become uninhibited and mean-spirited because the internet can give us the ability, in many cases, to remain anonymous. Through this anonymity, it gives us more encouragement to say what we really feel or influence the thoughts and actions of others. There is cyberbullying and stalking, there is racist ranting, name-calling, prejudice, belittling, anger, and much more.

So, is the internet promoting less physical and emotional connectedness and more dishonest discourse? Yes, in some cases, where people feel distant and physically removed from others, it may further enhance whatever behavior is present in their hearts and minds. In defense of the internet and social media, these platforms also give us instant access to the maladies and afflictions that affect people both domestically and globally. It is sometimes through this "instant knowledge" that we will participate in a cause, or provide monetary assistance (gofundme.com, for example) and support to whomever or whatever. Here, the internet can be used to exert kindness and help strangers who we may never meet.

The economy is yet another factor that may influence our future capacity to be kind. As our economies become more global and interconnected, there will be successes and failures, and the competition for limited resources, both natural and manmade, may become fierce. Some countries will rise, and some will fall along with the well-being of their respective populations.

This will cause a chasm between wealthier and poorer countries and can germinate the seeds of war and its proliferation if not addressed or mitigated. Here in the US, the aftershocks of COVID-19 resulting in joblessness, poverty, and inflation, are still pushing people over the edge, and they are angry. Even if you were working during the height of the pandemic, you faced ongoing job uncertainty, or were touched to some degree by a personal monetary shortfall (i.e., lost, or reduced wages, shrinking 401(k), etc.). All of this has produced a continuous widening gulf between those who have and those without. It will be imperative that we all find a way to assist those who may have fallen into hard times, if possible. It is important to both our species and our very existence. Through our kindness, compassion, courage, and actions, we can begin to positively transform the lives of others by elevating their current state of being and state of mind.

Another vexation is polarized politics and the dehumanizing and devaluing of those who do not believe as we do: tribalism. We keep finding ways to separate ourselves from others and blame one another based on political ideology, race, religion, or ethnicity. Our very survival as humans will be predicated on continuously finding ways to connect while maintaining our individuality, not divide. As John Dickinson, one of The Founding Fathers of the United States, famously and prophetically penned, "United we stand, divided we fall," in his tune, "The Liberty Song." We can either unite or fall. Because of our questioning nature, it is foolish to expect everyone to reach a consensus on everything; however, the more we interact and tear at the walls of ignorance and bias and recognize the overwhelming similarities we possess, the greater our ability to be kind toward others. This will help us to advance and survive as a species. Kindness should also extend to helping our planet heal and reinforce our dedication to ensuring the continued existence and proliferation of other species. If only mankind, womankind, and childkind become kind men, kind women, and kind children, we can transform our future both collectively and individually.

I see a future of hope and endless possibilities to right-size humanity and the world in which we live, and the crowning achievement of this will materialize through our uniting in selflessness and courage.

> *"If we surrender to and practice compassion towards one another, our future is secure."* ~J. Touché

CHAPTER 15

KINDNESS AND TECHNOLOGY

Technology, like the future of kindness, needs its own area of exploration because it shapes the future. Humans will always interact with each other in some capacity; however, the future—like human nature—is unpredictable, and with this, at what level will kindness display itself? Will technology, with all its marvels to connect us "electronically," become a double-edged sword in that it will also serve as the primary impediment to our being able to feel, touch, hear, smell, verbalize, and more, with other humans? Will we be relegated to becoming a digitized pixel image on a computer screen, further separating us from one another and, perhaps, reality as in artificial intelligence (AI)? We must be vigilant in ensuring that we make it a top priority to stay physically connected; otherwise, we face desensitization and, through the lessening of emotion, grow into a society of waning feelings, where both life and death will become 'just another uncelebrated event' devoid of importance. And, with this minimization of feelings, the slow anemic atrophy of kindness, compassion, and more importantly, love. There are studies showing that we are less empathetic or kind and more self-centered than at any time in decades. Dacher Keltner, PhD, of the University of California, Berkeley, says that we are a "touch-deprived" culture: "We need more mindfulness, more contemplation, and more gentle reassuring holding of hands. The survival of the kindest depends on it."

When you keenly observe some interactions between people, you can sense or feel the meanness in the world on the increase, as mentioned at the beginning of this book. The pandemic exacerbated hostility in some people as they were forced to stay home, social distance, and cope with the disruption to their treasured way of life. Some may argue that this meanness has always been there, but through Twitter (now X), Facebook, Google, TikTok, Instagram, left-wing media, right-wing media, and social media in general, these tools bring this ugliness into our focus and collective minds almost instantaneously. The question remains: Are we rushing toward our own demise—instantly? Only through kindness, love, courage, and compassion will we advance or survive as a species.

I believe in a kinder, gentler future, where we grow together for the common good rather than farther apart. I hope, for the sake of generations and civilizations to come, that we leave them a legacy where we made giant strides toward embracing our differences for the sake of peace. Our future rests on the children of today and how we help them deal with wars, pandemics, civil unrest, global economic instability, unemployment, political squabbling, poverty, and hunger, through the examples we set, for they are watching. I believe we have the courage to unite; we now need its manifestation.

CHAPTER 16
KIDS AND KINDNESS

It takes very little effort to be cruel or mean. In our schools, we see kids bullying other kids—sometimes to the point of suicide. My own experience with a bully happened when I was in elementary school. There was this kid named R. C.; he was my boogeyman, and not some specter that appeared in my dreams. He was my waking "Freddy Krueger" because it seemed as if every time I turned around, he would be somewhere near and menacing. Now, I was not looking for trouble. I thought I was a nice kid in that I did not pick fights, did not talk about others behind their backs, did not run with a wild crowd, did not do anything that would raise the ire of someone, had lots of friends, so, I could not understand why R. C. would threaten me for what seemed like an everyday occurrence—and without reason. I went out of my way to avoid him, and he always talked tough around the other kids, hauling around this 'attitude' or "chip on his shoulder" wherever he went.

One day while we were in the gym, he purposely moved right behind me in line and started speaking in a low, threatening tone in my ear so that the teacher would not hear him. For some reason, still unknown, I spun around and hit him. It was not planned; it was an uncharacteristic reaction that even surprised me because when I connected my fist to his jaw, he stumbled about seven feet backward, landing against the mats hanging on the walls and slowly slid down, resting in a sitting position with his legs spread apart. An eerie silence filled the room in what is usually the noisiest class in the school. I was afraid that he would get up and continue our fight; however, he sat there for a few minutes, staring blankly toward the floor, stunned, and rubbing his jaw. The other kids were afraid of him, too, and when they saw him on the ground with one punch, they lost their fear of him.

After that day, neither I nor any of the other kids ever had a problem with R.C., and for a long time, kids in our school would come up to me and remind me almost heroically about the "Batman" punch that leveled one of the most feared bullies in our school. I do not advocate violence in any form, nor do I condone hurting others, but I was young and did not have the mental toughness or knowledge to dismantle R.C. without striking him. But this one act gave me great courage that has stuck with me my entire life in that I am not afraid of bullies and have and will always stand up to them.

At the core of a bully is a coward who bluffs his or her way into having others fear them. Do not allow bullies to sense that you fear them because fear feeds their egos and encourages them to act out. As it was then, some of today's kids consider it fashionable to put other kids down, or instill fear and ridicule them, as R.C. had. In a society where strength is equated with showing bravado and aggression, there is little wonder as to why kids who are kind or nice, non-combative, or seekers of peace, become the target of bullies. In the mind of the bully, they are weak and feel their will can be imposed on them. Sometimes the bully will enlist others to "gang up" on these kids, further ostracizing, alienating, and deepening this fear.

Believe it or not, there is kindness in everyone, including the bully. But, when society relishes and promotes aggression and domination, this kindness and empathy dissipates into meanness, and bullying becomes the norm. What would happen if a kid expressing concern and courage stood up for the one being bullied? They would find themselves the target of the same bully, and maybe worse because they had the moxie to speak out against injustice.

Kindness takes courage because it is rooted in universal love, respect, truth, and doing what is right. Some would argue that "right" is a subjective term that is either good or bad depending on the way in which it is defined by either the participant or observer. I say right is that which leads to or is intended for a positive outcome or a win-win for both parties. We must raise our children to respect and care for others and nurture them in such a way that whether we are present or not, they will make strong, affirmative choices. It is the lack or reduction of this nurturing that sometimes leads children to make their own choices, or become bullies, and in the young brain, rationalization is still immature and developing. This part of the brain, the prefrontal cortex, matures last. By training children, patiently, persistently, and most importantly, lovingly, what they learn and do becomes mantra-like, not robotic, and may serve as instinctual mapping for the choices they make.

There are studies which show where parents value their children's achievements over having empathy for others. As parents, we should be equally concerned that our children embrace both and become creative, accomplished, and compassionate individuals. Few cannot recall the story of *Frankenstein*. According to the original book by Mary Wollstonecraft Shelley, Victor Frankenstein created a creature from body parts and gave it a brain. We have been misled through the movie industry that the "monster" had a criminal's brain and Frankenstein was a doctor—both untrue. His creation was kind, humble, very intelligent, and taught himself to read and speak French. The "creature," as he was called because of his hideous appearance, like Joseph Carey Merrick, a.k.a., "The Elephant Man," frightened people, and they were mean to him as a result. The book further points out that the creature sought friendship from the patriarch of a family named DeLacey near their cottage where he had been out looking for food.

While the family is away, the creature slips into the home and befriends Mr. DeLacey. Being blind, he listens to the creature's tale of mistreatment and the misery of his origin and does not pass judgment on him. Through his blindness, he hears the humility and kindness in the creature's words. Mark Twain says, "Kindness is the language which the deaf can hear and the blind can see." And, in this case, it was true. However, the family returns and sees the creature and how ugly he appears, so they drive him from their home and back into the forests. He later shares with his creator, Victor Frankenstein: "I was benevolent and good; misery made me a fiend. Make me happy, and I shall be virtuous." Frankenstein further rejects the creature: "Begone! I will not hear you. There can be no community between you and me; we are enemies. Begone, or lest us try our strength in a fight where one must fall." The creature appeals to him again for kindness and compassion; "I was benevolent; my soul glowed with love and humanity: but am I not alone? ...You, my creator, abhor me; what hope can I gather from your fellow creatures who owe me nothing? They spurn and hate me. ...These bleak skies I hail, for they are kinder to me than your fellow human beings."

Like the "creature" in Shelley's book, our children cry out to us for help—you created me, yet you pay no attention to me, the kids at school are mean to me, you do not listen when I tell you these things, all I want is to be loved and to feel safe. Perhaps, this is why some kids go astray and to extremes, such as what we saw in the Newtown, Connecticut, mass shooting. They call out to us for help, and we fail them. While at school, they are bullied, teased, and the subject of gossip and ridicule because of how they look, dress, act, or speak. When they are home, we as parents are so busy or preoccupied that we do not spend time with them as with the Oxford High School shooter more recently. They are miserable and lonely. As the creature said to his creator, Victor Frankenstein— "I was benevolent and good; misery made me a fiend. Make me happy, and I shall be virtuous." They try and make friends and are shunned or attempt to be kind or compassionate and are met with scorn and ridicule, or they are "different" or extremely introverted, and become stereotyped. They do not want to be miserable; they want to be happy; they want to be enveloped in love; they want to feel that someone genuinely cares for them when they walk through the door and their parents are there to listen and support them.

While we cannot make anyone happy, we can listen. And through our listening, we show kindness, concern, and respect to these kids; we give them the attention they need and once they trust that someone really cares about them, they can be made 'virtuous and benevolent' once more.

Think back to your own childhood. Maybe you were bullied or picked on, as I was, or observed others who were. Perhaps you were the bully. Then you partially understand the challenges that kids face while in school today, and I say partially, because when some of us were in grade school, junior high, or high school, the internet did not exist, neither did tablets, smartphones, or prepaid phones—just communication via face-to-face, landline phone, or through the written word. Back then if you were bullied, it usually happened on the playground, cafeteria, or after school and in person. With the rapid advancement of communication technologies, these bullies can now come into your home by way of wireless and "cyberbully" kids without the parents ever knowing it. Unfortunately, you cannot come home and escape it anymore—the threats, the taunts, and insults. Experts lay part of the blame on the technological changes in our society. The anonymity of the internet allows all kids to be cruel if they choose.

Our daughter came home from school one day and shared a story about a kid who had been bullied at her school. She said the kid was 'different,' had a foreign-sounding name, and that he was somewhat eccentric—which caused him to stand out from the other students. She went on to say that other kids, mostly boys, had taunted and teased this kid and it made him act out even more. My wife and I were immediately alarmed by this revelation. Have these kids not heard of Columbine? This is not to say that every kid who is bullied or ridiculed will become violent or vindictive; but the possibility of some future trauma involving this kid has been elevated.

Both kindness and cruelty manifest themselves in many ways; a child who is kind to animals will more than likely be kind to people. You can almost predict that a kid who is cruel to their pets or other animals will also show the same cruelty toward people. An exceptional example of this was that of Jeffrey Dahmer, a convicted serial killer. According to the Animal Legal Defense Fund, as a child, Dahmer would catch and torture animals such as dogs, cats, and frogs. The ALDF also cites other well-known killers of humans who mistreated and abused animals in their early backgrounds, such as Albert DeSalvo ("Boston Strangler"), Ted Bundy, Patrick Sherrill (who killed 14 coworkers at a post office), Dennis Rader ("BTK Killer"), Andrew Cunanan (who murdered fashion designer Gianni Versace and four others), and David Berkowitz ("Son of Sam"). This is not to say that all kids who show cruelty toward animals will grow up to be serial killers or mass murderers, but we must teach them the importance of life—from the lowest to the largest creature. Children need to be taught kindness to animals, period, and we have an obligation to guide them toward better, more humane relations with all living things.

CHAPTER 17
YOU WERE BORN OUT OF KINDNESS

The one universal truth is we are born and will eventually die. How we are born, where we are born, and when we are born are all unpredictable, as is when, where, and how we will die. But why we were born is because of God's kindness. It was God who allowed us to be born, and through his kindness, we lived. This is not to say that once we are born, we are delivered into kindness. We are all born into our own unique circumstances—some favorable; some not. Some of us arrived with the love of two parents, some with the love of one parent, and others with the love of neither. My wife and I have three healthy children, and we loved them long before they arrived.

Many of you arrived on this Earth with similar parental love and anticipation. I completely admire the parent and parents who have been told that their child would be born with a disability or other complications, and yet they allow the baby to be born. But not only this, they love their newborn as much as they would love a healthy child and are prepared to take care of it and raise it to be as normal as possible. It did not matter about the state of the child, only that it was theirs and they were there to love it. I have also seen the other side of being born into the world where the child arrived unwanted, or where the parents were not equipped to take care of the child. It could have been due to the young age of the birth parent, addiction, mental illness, parental abandonment, or it was an unexpected birth.

A few years back, after we had raised our two oldest children, my wife and I decided to try and help give a child who had been born into a precarious situation a chance to be loved and to know what it was like to have a family. We found a child who was in his mid-teens and had been featured in our local newspaper. He wanted a family; he wanted to live outside the city, to travel, to have his own room and space, and a dog. We thought, wow, we could provide all of this, and we had an extra room where he could enjoy his privacy! What was most uncanny is that he could have passed for our biological son, in that he looked like us. So, we went through all the state-mandated training, background checks, home inspections, licensing, etc. After months of preparation, we were finally ready to welcome this young man into our family and were very excited. Initially, he was allowed to come visit our home and spend a few days, then weeks, and finally returned to his current foster parent.

Over time, it became apparent that he did not like following rules and was adept at using his unfortunate circumstances to elicit sympathy from adults so that they would give him whatever he wanted without him reciprocating by "doing the right thing." Maybe he never learned what it meant to obey rules or to have discipline, and that was paramount to living in our home. Disappointingly, it did not work out. We were prepared and willing to do whatever it took to give him the family, love, kindness, encouragement, and educational support that he may not have ever had. We could see that he was highly intelligent and personable, but he was also very manipulative, perhaps due to survival instincts he had developed in the foster care system and used his naturally sweet outward disposition to achieve the outcomes that he desired.

He was born into neglect and poverty, and had he received a more nourished upbringing, he could have been genuinely kinder and more caring. This "nourishment" could have come in the form of a loving relative, a caring teacher or caseworker, or anyone who values you and you trust them in return. You can still be sincerely kind or nice regardless of past or current circumstances. While you cannot choose your parents, you can choose or learn to be kind and find the courage to overcome the conditions into which you were born. You were born out of God's kindness, and through his mercy and blessings, you can find purpose, happiness, and love.

CHAPTER 18

HOW KINDNESS WENT TO THE SIDELINES

Somehow the notion of "mine" entered our collective being, and with it, the need for self-gratification began to outweigh the good of the whole. We became critically self-centered and focused on our titles, occupations, and having more "stuff" than anyone else, to help fill the void of insecurities on our jobs, in our love lives, relationships with our parents or siblings, with friends, religious purpose, our past, or whatever. Due to these uncertainties, many things that have traditionally involved helping or being kind to others went by the wayside. The increased condensation of "affluenza" created the perfect storm for replacing "we" with "me." How many times have you heard, "It's all about me?" Some people have gone as far as wearing self-promoting clothing proclaiming this boast.

With the advent of this feeling of entitlement, grandiosity, and self-importance, reaching out, reaching back, or reaching down to help someone up took a back seat. If something did not benefit us directly—whether financially, physically, or emotionally—it became less important to show kindness or concern for the person or matter at hand. Peer pressure to conform also contributed to this way of thinking. We tend to equate having money with happiness, leaving us feeling unfulfilled in our pursuit of materialism. People tied the correlation of happiness to the model of car we drove, where we worked, the neighborhood where we lived, the schools our kids attended, and the "influential" people we knew or considered as friends. It even trickled into where we attend church, synagogue, mosque, and temple. It was as though we were saying because you attend a certain religious institution composed of certain kinds of people, it could be confirmed that this reflected your values and status. Whether your religious institution was in an impoverished or a wealthy area also contributed to how you were "defined."

With so much focus on materialism, competition, and exclusivity, we lost our sense of kindness. If you ask a typical child in the US what they want to be when they grow up, in most cases it would be to become famous. Famous for doing what? Mostly, it is based on the images they see on television or the internet where famous people are always laughing, having fun, throwing, or attending lavish parties, living in huge homes, driving nice cars, being surrounded by "beautiful" or well-connected people. To be fair, you can also find children who want to someday develop a cure for cancer, erase poverty from the earth, and help people who cannot or are unable to help themselves. However, in many cases, the pursuit of wealth and "stuff" is perpetuated and ingrained by the parent, and the child is indirectly and subliminally led down the path of self-interest and self-absorption.

As a parent, I understand wanting my kids to attain or have more than I did, but first and foremost, I wanted them to know and understand where these "things" came from, or to constructively work toward a goal to obtain what they needed or wanted. We taught our children to be "good kids" and to grow up to be honest, respectful, and responsible. Some parents push their kids to do better, get more, have greater, by any means necessary and without regard to ethics, rather than encouraging them to focus on using their gifts to be honest, do good works, or to benefit others. True kindness and self-gratification cannot coexist. It is comparable to the biblical saying: "No man can serve two masters: for either he will hate the one and love the other...."

It is possible, however, to be kind, have wealth and be truly generous. I read an article about Harris Rosen, President and COO of Rosen Hotels and Resorts in Orlando, Florida. Like me, you have probably never heard of Mr. Rosen, but he started his hotel chain 50 years ago during the oil embargo, which had a devastating impact on the hotel industry in Central Florida. A New York native, he had worked at various hotels and resorts across the US, including Disney, and that is how he found his way to Orlando. Times were bad there in the early 1970s when he encountered the owner of a Quality Inn who desperately wanted to unload the hotel. Mr. Rosen bought it with $20,000—all the money he had in the world—and assumed a $2.5 million mortgage on a hotel with a "15% occupancy rate and hemorrhaging cash."

Afterward, he said, "I walked into my new office, put my head on my desk and cried, believing I had just done the dumbest thing in my life." Rather than wallow in despair, Mr. Rosen struck deals with motor coach companies along the East Coast to freeze the hotel rate for their passengers visiting Orlando and was met with kindness and support from the owners of these companies. After a few months, the hotel became profitable and Mr. Rosen became "the breakfast cook, the meat carver on the buffet at night, the gardener, the general manager, security director," and many other roles. It was through his hard work and God's blessings that he acquired another hotel, then another and others.

Mr. Rosen could have sat back and selfishly relished in his success, but he says, "It suddenly became clear that it was time for me to start giving back." So, he started the Harris Rosen Foundation, which provides funding for numerous philanthropic initiatives, opened a college at the University of Central Florida, and created a $5 million endowment fund, which provides 100 to 150 scholarships every year. He then went on to create the Tangelo Park Program in an impoverished neighborhood in Central Florida, and for the kids there, it provides fully paid vocational and college scholarships once they graduate from high school. Mr. Rosen has also endeavored to build local community centers to help the people of Haiti. Toward the end of this article, Mr. Rosen is quoted as saying, "Looking back, had it not been for those incredibly kind, gracious men and women who assisted me when I most needed it, we would not today have the means to offer our assistance to those who need a helping hand. We shall continue our philanthropic endeavors well into the future because we truly believe that giving back to others is the best investment we can ever make." How is that for a testimony of someone who does not hoard his wealth or seek self-promotion? Through his quiet and unassuming kindness and concern for others, Mr. Rosen strives to make the world a better place. His excellent example shows that you do not have to relinquish all your worldly goods and show piety or take a vow of poverty to practice kindness; it is the attitude and purpose behind your actions.

Dr. Dacher Keltner, University of California, Berkeley, pointed out that we have become less gentle toward each other, and I believe, in part, it is due to our increased self-centeredness. Just drive down the street and perhaps you pause to let someone into traffic. Eight out of ten times the person does not acknowledge through a wave or any other gesture, that you were thoughtful enough to give them a break. They sometimes will either not glance your way or give you a haughty look of indifference or entitlement with their noses in the air. Now, if you were to block them in and deny their entry into traffic, they flip you the finger, beep their horn, or fling their hands up in the air in an expression of "Why?" Kindness should work like this, too, in that you were doing something for the benefit of someone else—no strings, no expectations. Selflessness should be at the center of each kind act—do your kind deed whether the other person acknowledges it or not and move on to the next one.

Why is it that we sometimes as a society glorify the nastiness in the world? If you are a follower of US politics, you will see a great deal of deceit, rudeness, and one-purpose personalities. If you lived in the US during the 2012, 2016, and 2020 presidential elections, you would have noticed, based on historic television ratings, our primal need to see candidates' exact punishment in the form of extreme "ugliness" debate with each other. It was a spectacle right out of the ancient Roman Coliseum; two or more "political gladiators" verbally slugging it out in their quest to become president or get re-elected. The tone on both sides split the country in two and was further fueled by political PACs and left-wing and right-wing news outlets. Amazingly, the upcoming 2024 US presidential election is shaping up to far outdo the vitriol of all of these. It is on track to become the most divisive election in the history of our country; one with potentially monumental consequences for our democracy.

We have all heard or read the biblical passage stating, "Every kingdom divided against itself is brought to desolation; and every city or house divided against itself shall not stand." We, as a nation, must be very careful not to allow this to happen.

I had an opportunity to look at some of the debates from the early years of television and there are distinct differences between the debates of then and now. There was a time when there was a degree of civility between the candidate and the person serving in the Office of the President of the United States of America. All of that has changed. The political stage nowadays has become the equivalent of a reality television show in that anything goes, and nothing is off-limits, not even the family members of the President or candidates. More important and alarming, is what does this type of negative behavior, disrespectful and rude commentary teach our children? We can have as many forums, seminars, symposiums, retreats, and debates as we want to address bullying and bad behavior in our children, but when they see where it can be used to their advantage and is perceived by their young minds as "acceptable," why be kind? Be kind and achieve what? More problematic is when they see adults behaving this way, they may believe this is the correct way to interact with others. Children are always observing how we act, interact, and monitoring what we say. As adults, we become their barometers, and they will often imitate what they see. We must always, especially when children are present, try to model positive behaviors and integrity, and not let kindness and civility remain on the sidelines.

CHAPTER 19

THE CURSE OF KINDNESS?

Some people believe that their kindness is a curse. They think they are programmed to always draw them toward someone needing their help, or them serving as a "magnet" for those seeking assistance. Like some of you, I have had personal experiences where total strangers have come to me for help. In a more remarkable instance, my wife and I were on our honeymoon in New Orleans, Louisiana, and we decided to take a bus tour of some of the old, stately plantations. As we exited the bus, a man came up to me seemingly out of nowhere and said he was "told" that I could help him out and asked me to pray for him. So, I excused myself from my wife and went a short distance away from where the other tourists were departing the bus and asked him to kneel with me. I began to pray over him and asked that whatever problem was bothering him to leave. He started to cry uncontrollably and not wanting to embarrass him by asking what the nature of his problem was, I simply ended with "God Bless You." We embraced, and he told me how much he needed and appreciated my prayers. He was not what some would or should label as being a derelict, or outwardly suffering from mental illness, just someone seeking the prayers of a stranger to help him through his pain and misery.

When I look back to that moment, I know that I had shown kindness through my action, and that it could have only been God who had "told" him to seek me out. I could have become suspicious and brushed him off, or not trusting enough to venture too far from the crowd with this stranger or fearing that he was going to rob me of some material possession, or worse. I stepped out on faith that this man genuinely needed and wanted my prayers, and it took courage to stray from the "safety" of others. As quickly as he had appeared, he disappeared, and I could not even tell you to this day what he looked like, what he was wearing, or any other identifiable feature.

I truly believe that sometimes God sends us His angels, whether disguised as beggars, strangers in need or distress, to test our love of Him and others. He also wants us to use discernment or common sense to not deliberately put ourselves in danger. Stepping out on faith is one thing; stepping off a high cliff is yet another. Kindness is a blessing, not a curse, for you have been given something the world needs more of, and it is special!

CHAPTER 20
DISCERNMENT AND KINDNESS

T hroughout this book, I have given personal examples of kindness to strangers, kindness from strangers, and deception from those pretending to be kind or in need. As much as we may want to help others through our kind acts, it is imperative that we pray and ask for discernment. There are various definitions of discernment, and the example I will use here is being able to sense or surmise whether someone is truly in need of kindness or setting us up for a trap. Being kind also means not putting yourself in harm's way unnecessarily. I shared in another chapter where the serial killer, Ted Bundy, would feign disability and use the kindness of women to murder them. I also shared where a "needy" man tried to rob me while I was on crutches and after having given him money. These examples, and the ones that you have experienced yourselves, could make you fearful or hesitant about helping or showing kindness—especially to strangers.

We are each born with five senses—sight, smell, touch, hearing, taste—and their role is to communicate information or stimuli to our sensory organs. The major human sensory organs are the nose, eyes, ears, tongue, and skin, and each of these contains receptors. Receptors are defined as being a cell or group of cells that receive stimuli from sense organs. By using any combination of these sensory organs, based on the strength or clarity of the stimuli, we can transmit or communicate enough of this sensory material through their respective sensory neurons, then on to our brain for processing. Once received by our brains, this information helps us determine what something is, or could be, or is not. So, what about the low to absent external communications, where the signals or stimuli are faint or undetectable or undefined? Basically, the meaning behind the actions or words or body language of others may not be clear or immediate, and here, not enough signal strength or information is being transmitted to our sensory organs for our brains to decipher then act or react. Here, we must go even deeper to assess something, and this is the realm of discernment.

Sometimes in this instance is where our intuition or a "gut reaction," kicks in, alerting us to sense that "something does not feel right" about someone, or a situation. This intuition, or gut reaction, is then carried to the higher level of discernment, alerting you to hidden dangers, or preparation for a fight or flight response. At all times, we must be open to our intuition or initial impression. Altruism has its place in life, but it is also important to sense when and when not to enter a situation. There are countless stories about people who were kind or helpful who were taken advantage of or murdered.

I read in the news the story of an elderly retired gentleman who would make a three-times-a week pilgrimage to a restaurant where everyone knew him, and he, in turn, knew them. During one of his weekly visits, he was approached and "befriended" by a young, unknown woman who asked him if she could use his cell phone and, out of kindness, he complied. Afterward, she continued to talk with him. Then, suddenly, she swiped the keys to his vehicle and ran out of the restaurant. He closely pursued her, and when she jumped into his truck and he tried to stop her, she ended up running over him and kept on going. The woman, later identified as a heroin addict and mother of two, sold the truck for drugs, was arrested, and sentenced to life in prison for his murder.

This could have happened to any of us, and most people who are kind or concerned about others would have done the same as this man. There are questions that remain as to whether she gave off any verbal clues or body language that his sensory organs, discernment, or intuition would or could have picked up on, such as the constant eyeing of his keys because they must have been visible for her to have taken them. Or did she talk about having to get somewhere very soon? How did she happen to sit down with the elderly man, a total stranger, and what did they talk about before she took his keys? The news article alleged that she used his cell phone to call and meet with her drug dealer. Was he paying attention to any of this discussion? Was she acting nervous or sweating? Were there non-verbal, weak signals or clues given where he could have picked up on something not being quite right with this lady, or that there was more to her just sitting there talking with him? She must have seen him getting out of his truck, then followed him into the restaurant with the motive for carjacking him. This is where deploying our sensory organs along with discernment and intuition are invaluable.

Unfortunately, in today's world, we cannot blindly trust everyone, even with our kindest intentions. So, we must use all resources available—including prayer and having faith. As Jesus told his disciples: "Behold, I send you forth as sheep in the midst of wolves. Be ye therefore wise as serpents and harmless as doves."

I had a situation that happened years ago while living in Denver, which today makes me want to shake my head as to what I was thinking back then. I had moved into a new apartment and was dead tired. All I could think about was getting some sleep. It was nighttime, about 10:30 p.m. or so, and I had just begun to doze off. Suddenly, I heard cursing and the sound of items being tossed around in the apartment below. I initially attempted to ignore what was happening, thinking that whatever caused the fight would soon blow over. WRONG! In fact, the fight escalated to the point where I could hear a person, presumably a woman, being tossed around followed by loud wailing and "extreme" cursing. After nearly a half an hour of this, I had had enough, so I gathered up the courage, or foolishness, went downstairs, and knocked on the door to the apartment. The guy, who was at the center of the fight, came to the door and flung it open and was squarely looking at me and sweating profusely from his earlier activities. First, I attempted to disarm him by apologizing for coming to his apartment, then explained that I was extremely tired and lived in the apartment above theirs. I went on to tell him that whatever he did in his apartment was his business and that I only wanted to get some sleep. To my surprise, he apologized and said "they" would keep the noise down. I thanked him and returned to my place. After that, I could not hear a pin drop downstairs and fell fast asleep.

Any police officer will tell you that one of the most dangerous situations they routinely encounter is where there is a domestic disturbance, and here I am—no badge, nor gun, nor authority—entering this squabble. When I think about my actions today, I am blessed that this guy did not have a gun; did not turn his anger toward me, or worse. If I had to do it all over again, I would have either called the police or the apartment manager—not endangered my life. Maybe I saved the life of the battered woman that night by intervening—however foolish my actions. To be honest, I did not enter this situation using either discernment or common sense, as my being extremely tired clouded my judgment. That is why I would advise you to pray constantly for the spirit of discernment, because having courage, or being kind, without God's protection, could lead to your detriment or demise.

CHAPTER 21

WHAT IS YOUR KIND IQ?

Zero! That is right, zero! Your kindness or capacity to be kind cannot be measured quantitatively or qualitatively. It is an action that happens without prediction and is mostly spontaneous; therefore, it comes, then dissipates. Dr. George Price, the great American geneticist and genius, attempted to measure human altruism and created the "Price Equation," which postulates the more similar an organism is to another, the more that organism will be inclined to be altruistic toward it. Through natural selection, the organism will be more likely to save the gene pool closest to its own. In doing this it showed that the organism is self-serving and not altruistic in that it is attempting to ensure that its genes survive and carry on. Dr. Price became disillusioned by his findings that true altruism did not exist, and he could not prove it mathematically.

He set out to disprove his own equation—so much so that he eventually became an "altruistic" patron of the downtrodden in the London neighborhood where he lived at the time. Dr. Price felt such compassion toward the alcoholic men in the area that he opened his home to them—showing them kindness. Eventually, the men stole from him, he lost everything he had: his home, and more tragically—his family. Despondent, he committed suicide. Kindness, like altruism, is like a moving target and because of its randomness, factors not immediately present can influence its outcome. Therefore, it is almost impossible to measure.

CHAPTER 22
VISUALIZATION AND KINDNESS

Before you go out into the world today, envision yourself helping at least one person through kindness. It could be opening the door for someone, helping a kid whose ball has rolled into the street, saying a kind word, or trying to get along with that "hard to deal with coworker." Or maybe assisting your elderly or widowed neighbor clean up where the snow or leaves have accumulated. However trite these actions may appear to some, they are acts of kindness because they offered you nothing in return, and you did them willingly. Visualization is important for those who practice kindness because it reaffirms that your actions have purpose. Without visualization, mankind could not have imagined flying, creating a submarine, or building the pyramids. You get it; we must first see ourselves performing the act and believing it if it is to be achieved.

CHAPTER 23
PRAYER, FAITH, AND KINDNESS

All sincere kindness is of God, as is all life. Now, the person exhibiting kindness may or may not be of God because He uses people all the time to exert His will. Just as ancient biblical text shows, God used false prophets and a "lying spirit" who were not of Him to deliver His message to King Ahab. When the act of kindness is from someone of God, and they are of Him, through discernment you will know. Not always immediately, but by monitoring their words and actions. Do their words match their actions? Are they smiling in your face while trying to stab you in the back? Are they unethical or vindictive? Do they acknowledge or honor God?

We all have our doubts at times, and mostly this doubt is due to a lack of faith. We are afraid or doubtful that our kindness will help someone, or through our kindness, matters may be made worse. Before I started writing this book, I asked God to guide my heart, mind, and hand and that He would allow me to be truthful in sharing my experiences and wise in imparting knowledge. I prayed for His wisdom and instruction, and each time before I sat down to write and thereafter, I would pray. Was I afraid when tackling the subjects of kindness and courage? Absolutely, because it opened me up to a great deal of self-reflection—good and bad! But, through prayer, I knew He would provide me with inspiration, and I gained the courage to overcome this fear and doubt.

We are all on a journey and along the way have met people who, through kindness, we have helped or have helped us, and we remember fondly those who unselfishly gave of themselves freely and without any strings or attachments. God is kindness; He is love, He is mercy, and He is forgiving. He has given us a direct way to communicate with Him, and that is through prayer. So, the next time before you are called upon to show kindness, especially if you feel any fear, say a short prayer, if nothing more than, "Guide me, Father." The doubt that you may have had will leave you because He will give you the necessary courage and guidance. This transforms into faith, and with the faith of a mustard seed, you can begin to move mountains. With this faith, envision your act of kindness helping someone. Whether you ever receive a thank you, you are operating at the highest level in the universe—the spiritual realm. In this realm, you are not alone and here, all things are possible. Prayer also keeps us focused. Throughout the day you may hear people saying mean things or witness them committing unkind acts, and if you are weak in faith, you may also become caught up in this type of behavior. So, how do you keep your kindness intact? Through prayer!

You must pray for strength and clarity of mind and spirit—you must constantly try to be in this world, but not of it. Yours is a higher calling, not that you are better than others because we are all imperfect; however, to reap the highest fulfillment of spiritual blessings, you must, as much as possible, try and remain chaste. To gain further strength and reinforcement, surround yourself with people who are on a similar path of goodness; together you may be able to support each other—especially when one's spiritual fortitude or faith is failing, and doubt starts to set in. A twined rope is difficult to cut, but a strand alone shall perish.

While driving home the other evening, I noticed the marquee in front of a well-known national restaurant chain that made me slow down and reflect on a very busy highway. It simply read, "Pray for peace and kindness," and I began to think about this book. I also thought, "How powerful and necessary in today's world!" Sometimes it seems as if we have lost sight of these three words — prayer, peace, and kindness — and it is because we have lost faith. To lose faith is to feel hopeless. We have wars, like in Ukraine and Israel, going on all around us; the fear of nuclear war and pandemics, civil unrest, mass murders, negative social media posts and videos, robberies, carjackings, racial hatred, police killings, rape, identity theft, and an assortment of other sordid activities and conditions which add to our feelings of hopelessness. Faith, however, cannot inhabit the same space as fear. They are "polar opposite" and if you have faith, it is not that you are void of fear, but rather you manage it and do not let it creep into your spiritual space. Your spiritual space is where God dwells and works his wonders through our faith.

Because we are human, fear constantly tries to occupy the space where faith exists. Some of us have become apathetic or numb to the goings-on in the world because we feel as if we cannot control what is happening. This is where prayer comes in; it renews our faith and gives us hope, and because we have hope, it works with faith to minimize our fears and bring us peace. Many people are homeless, or depressed, suicidal, or scared because they have lost faith in ever being able to rise above their current situation. Perhaps it has been a long time since someone told them they can overcome this or helped them to believe in possibilities. That is where kindness can make a difference. When coupled with faith, hope, and prayer, it may be the perfect combination of positive energy to move them beyond where they are in their lives. And you just might be that needed catalyst.

CHAPTER 24

OH, GOODNESS!

Goodness essentially means being of good character. If you carry yourself in an upright way, if you have high moral standards, if you have integrity and honesty, you may be considered as possessing "goodness." Kind people are set apart in both word and deed, and because of this, people confide in them, share deeper thoughts, and develop trust in them. There are deceptively "kind" people, or kind/phony people, as mentioned earlier in the book, who will try and execute good deeds, not for the benefit of others but for themselves. Just like companies will jockey to be number one or show how their product is superior to that of their competitors, these people also try to appear pious, good, and godly, but either their words or actions will trip them up and expose their true intentions.

It is important for kind people to first be sincere and secondly, as much as humanly possible, be virtuous, not perfect! It is not always easy because there will always be temptation and roadblocks put in your way to test you. You must find a way to break through these barriers, not merely going around them. Jesus did not avoid the Pharisees; he challenged them and showed that even when faced with death, he would not give way to hating or harming them. He wanted to change their hearts and minds, not destroy them. Seek goodness, pray for it, and be of good character because at the very essence of good people is God.

CHAPTER 25
KINDNESS AND HEALTH

The first act of kindness should start with being kind to yourself. This means taking care of health needs—mentally, physically, emotionally, and spiritually. I have always struggled with my weight, and as I grew older, I was not active enough through sports as I had been to burn off many of those extra calories created by my intake, and the weight came. So, I decided to eat better, exercise more, rest more, and let stressful people and trivial things go. This past year, I rewarded myself by installing an organic garden in my yard. Growing vegetables and berries gave me a greater attachment not only to the earth but to the concept of farming, such as our ancestors did for survival. The same vegetables that I raised, I was now eating—no pesticides, chemicals, or nonorganic fertilizers. I have had a long, inhospitable history when it came to eating vegetables, but when the garden arrived and I tasted them, I fell in love with eating fresh produce. I discovered that a "better me," in terms of eating healthier, was growing right along with the yield from the garden.

After spending countless hours pulling weeds, watering, staking, and removing harmful insects, my mood changed. Being in the garden proved to be therapeutic and healthy in many ways: it was a form of low-impact exercise, gave me time to think and reflect, and sharpened my mental acuity along with reducing stress. Most importantly, it enhanced my spirituality because I felt that both the earth and God spoke to me while there. This transformation helped give me the motivation to continue to try and eat better, and I am still on the path. Being kind to yourself means giving back to yourself and spirit. You cannot help others if you cannot help yourself. If you are to be effective during your journey here on Earth, it begins with taking care of your health. The world needs more kind people, and if you leave it prematurely, a little less kindness will be around to do God's work.

As you must never give up on being kind, likewise, you must have the courage to be healthy, watch your weight, fend off depression, minimize stress, increase physical activity, avoid, or manage the "poisonous people" in your life, constantly find ways to improve yourself, and pray for strength and guidance. I have shared my health struggles with you and how I am confronting them. How about you; what are you doing with your own health? Your kindness is needed—and it starts within you.

> *"What does the Lord require of you but to do justice, and to love kindness, and to walk humbly with your God?"*
> ~Micah 6:8 (KJV)

CHAPTER 26
WHY KINDNESS SHOULD BE OUR LEGACY

We must all face the reality that we are mortal and that our time here on Earth is limited. Sometimes I think about how I would like to be remembered upon my own demise and how I would want my obituary to be read. I can think of no greater wording or legacy than, "He was a kind and compassionate man." That would trump my university education and training, my professional achievements, my possessions or how much money I had earned, who my friends were or organizations to which I belonged. Have you thought about your own legacy? What will be said of you? What intrinsic quality or qualities will you leave behind that sums up who and what you were while you were here?

I read an excerpt from Dr. Martin Luther King, Jr.'s, "The Drum Major Instinct," where he summarized how he wanted to be remembered. Dr. King essentially said he wanted to leave a "committed life" behind and all the trappings and luxuries of life did not matter. How profoundly selfless: "to leave a committed life behind!"

I thought about the many times when I had read someone's obituary where it only talked about the "surface" of that person—mother, father, employee, owner, son, daughter, friend, grandmother, grandfather, residence, niece, nephew, education, social or country club affiliation, activities, religion, etc. What about them on a deeper level; what did they do that set them apart? From a philosophical perspective, how would one epitomize the existence of their essence? I see kindness in:

"...she leaves a wonderful legacy behind—unconditional love and loyalty...."

"...she was an avid flower and vegetable gardener. She always made sure you left with flowers or vegetables...."

"...he never met a stranger. He made everyone feel welcomed as a friend...."

"...he was an advocate for developmentally disabled adults...."

How wonderful!

I also remember while growing up hearing or reading that the "good die young" or as the ancient Greek saying goes: "Whom the gods love, die young" and being totally perplexed by these statements. Having also been raised in a religious household, I had always believed the wicked would be "cut off," or "Honor thy father and thy mother: that thy days may be long upon the land which the LORD thy God giveth thee." Along the way, I often thought about the good and kind people that I knew, then the wicked or bad people—not judging, just observing their actions—that I had known. I began to see that many of the wicked were "cut off" due to their own vices and predicaments they had put themselves into, but the good and kind people were also dying or had died at a greater rate. Again, my intentions are not to sit in judgment of anyone here, but I felt it unfair that wicked people were living longer than the good.

I lost my father, whom I considered a good and kind man, to brain cancer when I was 12 years old, and he was 42. In my young mind, I surveyed some of the "wicked people" in my neighborhood — those who were cheating on their spouses (yes, kids in the neighborhood knew), exhibiting habitual drunkenness, and raising havoc. Worst of all were those who physically abused their children; I knew of them, too. Ironically, many of those same "wicked people" lived well into their 60s, 70s, 80s, and a few into their 90s, adding to the confusion over why my father had died so young while the wicked lived on.

Biblically speaking, had he been disobedient to his own mother or father? I began to rationalize that these good and kind people may have had shorter earthly lives, but they were more fulfilling and enjoyed an eternity of bliss in the afterlife. Whereas the wicked were left to live on and wallow in their own misery here on Earth and inherit God's wrath at Judgment when they died. This belief stuck with me in that I believed that a shorter, kinder life was more meaningful than a long wicked one, and that the kindness and goodness of a person will live on, even after death, because they will be remembered fondly for the "light" they brought into the lives of those they touched. This, in turn, made me think it was a far better legacy to be remembered for your qualities of kindness and "good works" than for that of wickedness. Therefore, a legacy of kindness will trump all that you have amassed in life; all the degrees and achievements you have acquired, all the status and honors that have been heaped upon you by others, all the material possessions you have gained, or the well-heeled people who you knew or rubbed elbows with while alive. Guard your legacy as closely as you would guard your own soul because they both will live on long after you have physically left the planet—for better or for worse.

CHAPTER 27

KINDNESS: OUR ENVIRONMENT AND OTHER SPECIES

As humans, we are the caretakers of our world. God put man and woman in charge of its maintenance and gave us dominion over all living creatures. Of the nearly nine million species that exist on land and in our seas, we are the only ones made in His image. Our religious texts were written neither for ape nor apricot but for mankind as a spiritual guidebook as to how we should conduct ourselves as the planet's closest personification of the Creator. As His custodians, we should show kindness toward the environment and other living creatures.

The Earth has experienced some phenomenal weather changes within the past three to four decades, and this is threatening the continued existence of many species—from pandas to polar bears. There is also some form of pollution everywhere. I was out in the middle of the Gulf of Mexico vacationing a few years back and could not believe that hundreds of miles from land I would see plastic balls, strips of foam-like materials, and other objects floating in the water. According to some research, fish and other mammals will many times eat these items or get entangled in man-made nets and die. We must be kinder toward our environment and protect other species so that future generations can enjoy them as much as we do today.

On a more land-based level, how many times have you seen people simply toss their trash onto the ground? Or you picked it up, only to return later and see it back again. I am sure at least three or more times a year. Looking at this problem from a global perspective: as of November 2022, the Earth had a population of approximately 8 billion people, of which 65% were between the ages of 15 and 64, or 5,161,478,750. If 20% of these 5.1 billion threw their trash on the ground, that would be the equivalent of 1 billion people polluting. Multiplying this number by three, we would have an estimated 3 billion incidents of trash tossing annually. What percentage of this trash will end up in our lakes, rivers, streams, oceans, fields, highways, or even outside of our homes? We must consistently practice environmental kindness because as the earth goes, so does mankind.

CHAPTER 28
KINDNESS AND ATTITUDE

You cannot be effectively kind if you have a negative outlook. From my perspective, and maybe yours, the first thing you do not want to hear in the morning is someone complaining about anything. The more extreme people will complain about everything! They dump on you and, if you allow them, will rob you of whatever energy or rejuvenation you may have accumulated overnight through rest or relaxation. If you hang around a negative person long enough, they will drain you. Or, worse, you may start to take on their characteristics. You might ask, "What if this person is my husband, wife, or significant other?" Then you must find a way to redirect their negative energy because that person is very close to you. You should be gentle, and just as firm, and let them know how their complaining or attitude is affecting you.

A negative person usually has a bad outlook on life or the things that are going on in their lives—either real or imagined. You will not convince someone who needs a hand that there is hope for them in their situation if they sense that you are wrestling with your own negative circumstances. They will look at you and say to themselves, "I may not have any money or be down on my luck, but I'm not miserable!" Negative people are usually miserable, and not all destitute people are unhappy—

they just lack financial resources, absence of support systems, or have low motivation. If you are truly positive in your attitude and your kindness reflects this, it may be just the spark to help uplift their spirits. Anything you attempt to do well in life will always begin with your attitude.

I remember fondly the famous poem called, "Thinking", by Walter Wintle, where he says success begins with your state of mind. Your attitude, or "state of mind," rubs off on those around you, and some are not aware of this fact. You know the adage: "Misery loves company"—it is true! Miserable people want to bring you into their misery, and I can honestly say that I have not met many, if any, miserable kind people. Kind people bring a different mindset in their approach to life—they live life; life does not live them. Again, they are victors and overcomers, not victims. Miserable people are victims because someone or something is always getting in the way of their happiness or success.

You cannot blame everyone or everything for your shortcomings, mistakes, or lack of planning. A lot of it comes from making poor decisions just as someone needing kindness or help may have also made bad choices in the past leading them to their current condition. You cannot lead others to higher ground if you are drowning in your own pond.

Another dilemma that kind people face is those who plot to exploit their kindness and compassion and try to take advantage of them. This can also affect the attitude of kind people, especially if they feel they have been "burned" in the past. They might consciously or subconsciously respond to this negative experience brought on by "users" by becoming skeptical, bitter, or apathetic toward the needs of others, therefore, less kind and trusting. As we have talked about previously, bitterness is an enemy of kindness. Depending on the "closeness" of the offender (i.e., sister, brother, aunt, uncle, best friend, etc.), the wound could run deep. That is why it takes practice and repetition to maintain your kind outlook and preserve your positive attitude.

As in sports, take pro golfers for example, their attitude and mental toughness will allow them to make better decisions and create more effective strategies. They may all have some degree of difficulty or problems in their personal lives off the course, but for them to win, they must always bring their "A" game each time and with every swing of the club. Kind people must do the same. Focus not on the past pain that you may have felt when someone tried to use you, but rather bring your very best to each day and to every situation. When you encounter these "users," take the lessons that you have learned in the past and head it off early in the interaction and regulate your attitude. Remember: "...be ye therefore wise as serpents and harmless as doves."

One important constant throughout your life is that you will always hear good and bad things about yourself—whether true or untrue. You cannot let the unkind words of others disrupt your kindness. Upon hearing negative things being said, you have many choices; you can lash out and confront the person who allegedly said something disparagingly about you, you can get angry and do nothing, you can sulk, you can turn inward for self-reflection or self-destruction, or you can take the high road and ignore their comments. You cannot allow others to infect, not affect, your attitude. If you do, you will need even greater courage to bounce back and not strike back. In a defensive mode, you cannot effectively do anything because eventually it will be revealed through either an action or a word. Keep your attitude in check, and as the Bible says, "Pray for those who spitefully use you and persecute you" and "The words of the reckless pierce like swords, but the tongue of the wise brings healing."

"Courage conquers fear and prepares the heart."
~ J. Touché

CHAPTER 29
WHEN KINDNESS AND ENABLING BISECT
HAVING THE COURAGE AND WISDOM TO ACT

In my journey to write this book, I asked a lot of people to share their perspective on kindness and the necessary courage it takes to be effective. One woman, a total stranger, who may have been in her mid-30s, told me enabling was at the center of her having to make a drastic decision a few months prior. She explained how her mother had come to live with her and became addicted to drugs. She said because it was her mother, she tried extra hard to show her kindness and understanding of her problem. She gave her mother her own room and money to spend, along with access to her car. However, her mother continued towards a downward spiral. This woman told me that when she had had enough, she asked her mother to leave. I am sure this was not an easy thing to do—to kick your own mother out, the one who gave you birth, the first eyes you gazed into when you arrived in the world. She said when she put her mother out, and she had to fend for herself, that is when she got the strength and resolve to become sober.

You may have experienced something like this in your own life, where you had a relative, a husband or wife, a child, friend, or colleague, who you tried to help get them back on their feet, or through a difficult situation, and found your efforts futile, leading you to gather the wisdom and courage to stop enabling them. Maybe it was not as drastic as that of the woman just mentioned, but something had to be done. If you have truly tried, unselfishly and lovingly, to help someone through sincere kindness, empathy, and understanding, then you should not feel guilty or blame yourself. You should be emboldened by your courage to act and wisdom to not become or remain an enabler.

Kindness should be as much about empowering and independence as it is about helping. Think about these two words for a moment—enabling and empowerment. While they share the same Greek roots, meaning "in" or "into," they produce different outcomes. Enabling encourages dependency and allows for repetitive behaviors; it creates a sense of security. If you have a pet and never let it out of a confined space, you are reinforcing your pet to become familiar exclusively with the surroundings you have introduced it to. Therefore, sometimes even with the door open, your pet will remain in that fixed space through conditioning and, perhaps, fear of the unknown. The pet is thus 'enabled' to stay confined in the house or indoors where everything is well-known and safe. Conversely, each time you let your pet outside to roam, your pet becomes more emboldened and will want to go out. In fact, our pets will sometimes jump around, scratch, or bark attempting to get our attention because they want to go out. They have become familiar with being outside, and you have empowered them to move comfortably from indoors to the outdoors.

When you enable someone, you trap them in their current state of being. This makes them dependent on you, and they will rely on you for assistance with anything deficient in their lives, such as money, sex, emotional state, comfort, drugs, alcohol, cigarettes, or whatever. Each time you give them what they want, not need, they feel "safe" and will continue to hang onto you. Unfortunately, this is sometimes to the detriment of the person providing these "wants" because they would not or could not empower these people to find their own way or satisfy their wants independently.

Kindness is not enabling because it is about helping people to eventually want to help themselves. It encourages them to move from the indoors to the outdoors and to become familiar with the unfamiliar because life itself is unpredictable, and tomorrow is unknown. If you are truly showing kindness to someone, you should also show them how to become self-sufficient; otherwise, you are enabling them. Who are you enabling, and why? Who are you empowering? Why are you afraid to act? How will you change this? Where is your wisdom and courage to act?

CHAPTER 30
KINDNESS, LOVE & RESPECT

First, you cannot be kind and not respect the person who is the intended recipient of your kindness, and you will love most the person who respects you. What do you remember about the kindness and affection you showered on the person you loved and respected? Love, kindness, and respect are connected, and should any one of these threads unravel, there goes the relationship and its longevity. Love is gentle, kindness is caring, and if the heart is sincere, the respect deepens. With this love and respect, kindness is born. Love is the mother of kindness, for without love, there would be no kindness. If we truly know how to love, or have experienced love, kindness will follow.

Be kind to your wife, your husband, significant other, parents, and children because if you really love them, they will feel it. Love is sometimes a feeling not spoken through words. You can tell someone you love them, but what do your actions say, and how do you make them feel? We have all heard or seen where a spouse or significant other is unkind, or in extreme instances, violent toward the very person they supposedly love. They will blame their actions on the person, some imagined circumstance like jealousy, or external factors, such as drugs or alcohol. To me, this is an excuse because if you truly love someone, you will first show kindness and respect toward them, and secondly, never ever deliberately hurt or wound them either physically, mentally, or spiritually.

We have all said or done hurtful things without thinking them through, but to be intentional or conscious in your actions says that your relationship is in serious trouble and should be reevaluated immediately. There is nothing worse than "loving" someone who you are also afraid of. In true love, there is no fear. Through trust, love blooms, and this is how you grow close; through fear is how you grow apart.

In the chapter, "Discernment and Kindness," I gave an example of where a man was literally beating a woman. I wonder what man would subject someone he loves to a beating, and what does physical punishment represent? Is it because he is angry about something totally unrelated and the woman is close by, so he uses her to release his warped emotions? Is he jealous of her, or a control freak? Did he grow up watching his father abuse his mother, as in a learned behavior?

On a personal level, during college, I briefly dated a woman who I treated with much respect—I never hit, berated, or even had a physical/intimate relationship with her. Our interaction, for me, was getting to know her. Months had passed and we continued dating until one day she told me that I must not care for her. This came as a total surprise to me. When I asked her why she felt that way, she replied, "Because we don't ever fight." This struck me as odd and I told her that I may argue, but I do not fight or hit women. Our relationship soured and in time we went our separate ways.

Years later, I ran into an old male acquaintance, and we were reminiscing about our college days, and somehow this young lady's name came up. It turned out that we had both dated the same person, but with opposing outcomes. He said, "She always wanted to fight" and was shocked when he told me how he had "obliged" her. This man told me how he would hit her and how she kept coming back at him. I lost respect for him at that moment but had wondered why she was like that. He filled me in on part of her background because he dated her much longer than I had. She had been abused by her biological mother who favored her sisters while growing up. As a result, she was "wounded." It then made sense as to why she wanted to fight and why if the person she dated did not hit, or fight her, she felt they did not love her. She had such low self-esteem that she felt only through violence or bloodshed could she be appeased or gratified. I do not know what became of this woman, but I pray that she sought and received the help she so desperately needed to ease her pain. I emphatically hope that my now former acquaintance has also gotten counseling for abusing her and thinking this type of behavior was somehow acceptable.

Biblically speaking, a man is supposed to love and care for a woman, and because Eve was made from Adam's rib bone, she in turn became part of him. If something comes from the rib bone, in most animals, it comes from its side. I advocate here that men should walk harmoniously with women—side by side as equals—not as inferiors, objects of sexual desire, "items" to denigrate, or punching bags—but as those who complete us as men. If a man truly loves the woman he is with, the greatest thing that man can do is to show her love, not just tell her. Always make each other feel loved and your union will be complete.

Lastly, to be fair, there are women who provoke their husbands, or significant others. They will emasculate them, show disrespect, curse at them and, in some instances, hit them. There are abused men out there, and this statistic is underreported due to social stigma— "A man is not supposed to get beat up by a woman." Estimates by the Centers for Disease Control (CDC) say one in seven men aged 18 and over in the US has been the victim of severe physical violence by an intimate partner in his lifetime. The CDC also says one in 10 men has experienced rape, physical violence, and/or stalking by an intimate partner. Women, if you love a man, as I told the men, show him, do not just tell him, and above all else, no violence! We should take the time, if allowed, to get to a deeper understanding of those we should love, respect, and show kindness toward.

CHAPTER 31
WOUNDED PEOPLE AND KINDNESS

There are wounded people in the world who were either unloved, unwanted, or abused when they were young, like the woman in the previous chapter. They grow up feeling like they do not need or want to show kindness to anyone. Or, sadly, they are so desperate for love and affection and kindness, they become the pawns of unscrupulous people who exploit them further. Low self-esteem, self-hatred, feelings of loneliness, despair, depression, or a me-against-the-world attitude is a constant reality for many wounded people. Perhaps wounded people think that everyone should be able to fend for themselves, like they had to, or they are in such a survival mode due to the way they grew up, they never learned or received much kindness. It is not that these people lack empathy; rather, they have dulled their emotions to love and kindness. Maybe they had to adopt this persona to muffle the pain of feeling unloved or rejected. This is also not to say that they are evil or mean-spirited, and it is not my intention here to pass judgment on them. I only wish that someone had taken the time or had the courage to show them love, compassion, and kindness.

I am sure that you know or have met one of these broken souls, and like you and me, they want to be happy. The next time you interact with someone like this, have the courage to show them that you care. You may initially encounter resistance because they have erected barriers to love and kindness over time, but eventually, if they feel your sincerity, they may let you in. Remember, love is not forceful; love is patient, gentle, and respectful. So, take things slow.

What if you are married to or dating a wounded soul? Well, it will require even more love and patience, and they must feel your genuineness; that you are in their corner and will be there for them. There is probably no greater pain than growing up as a child feeling unwanted or unloved to becoming an unwanted or unloved adult. In some cases, there will be a limit as to how much you may be able to do on your own to help them, and it could require the intervention of a mental health professional. Above all else, be real, be patient, support them, do not abandon them; they will eventually love and respect you for it.

"Kindness is the soul-salve which heals all wounds."
~ J. Touché

CHAPTER 32
KINDNESS, RACE, AND ETHNICITY

Race and ethnicity have and will always be topics that rise to the forefront of modern discussion— because we are a multiracial, multicultural nation and world. As humans, we are innately sensitive to others like us, just as animals interpret the sounds of like species to determine whether they are in distress or danger. Being of a higher order, we have been given greater reasoning abilities to ferret out information and assist in our decision-making.

We sometimes want to help "our own" in ways that divide along racial or cultural lines and in doing so, miss the true meaning of kindness because kindness, as justice should be, is "blind." It does not see differences in others; it sees commonalities. It seeks to resolve or assist in any way possible to limit suffering and encourages all to rise to the level of need. One of the greatest challenges faced by kind people will be their constant battle against succumbing to stereotyping. Kindness is one of the few qualities that triumphs over prejudice, and you will be told by others that "this group" or "those people," and on and on, are a certain way or have specific undesirable traits or customs because of their race, gender, ethnicity, sexual preference, disability, socioeconomic status, or religion.

Perhaps you were raised to believe this way, as some prejudice is taught to us as children by our parents, friends, or relatives and reinforced as adults. If so, you must break this cycle and refute this belief if you are to effectively practice kindness. People cannot be stroked with a broad brush; as unique to us as our fingerprints from that of any other human, so are our hearts, minds, and motivations.

When the Irish came to America, they were not treated well. They were predominantly poor because they were trying to escape the Great Potato Famine, a crop on which they had come to depend while in Ireland and scraped together what little money they had to sail to America. They were also predominantly Catholic and were looked upon with suspicion by their newly adopted Protestant country. In Ireland, Catholics were forbidden to own land or hold office, just to name a couple of the many barriers they faced. When they came to America, they arrived with the hope of gaining many of the freedoms that had eluded them in their native land, and they were wrong. Instead, what they found was more of the same discrimination that had made them leave Ireland in the first place.

In America, they were stereotyped as being lazy, pagan, alcoholics, and much more. As a group, they were treated with little kindness and denied access to many of the opportunities of the 19th and early 20th centuries. Like the Irish, along with African Americans whose ancestors were taken from Africa and forced into labor throughout North America, the Chinese and Latinos who helped lay the massive rail systems out West, Native Americans who were displaced when their land was taken, the Jews who faced severe anti-Semitism and restrictions upon their arrival, and countless other racial and ethnic groups, all sacrificed to help build America into the great nation it was to become, and still is. While some are still struggling to gain equality and respect, all these groups had to develop the fortitude to rise above their status and conditions.

What if we had embraced these people with kindness and acceptance early on? I truly believe that had we, our society would be further along the continuum of creating a positive and dynamic melting pot in which we could all comfortably call home. It takes courage to overcome current or past discrimination, but it takes kindness and patience toward all people to lift a nation or progress our species. Even as of the writing of this book, racial and ethnic strife, and unrest dominate America's headlines. It is time to confront and mend our past so that our children will inherit a kinder, more loving, and inclusive future.

While looking out of my window this evening, I saw the most beautiful crescent moon surrounded by a sea of stars. A clear, crisp night greeted my eyes, and it made me think of the religious symbol for Islam and, perhaps, our most talked about citizens, the Muslims. Few know that Muslims have been in America even before its founding, and many more arrived during the slave trade. I do not want to get political here, and some may disagree with what I am about to say, but we must unequivocally welcome Muslims as our brothers and sisters. At the beginning of this chapter, I talked about what a positive difference there could have been during the early formation of our nation had we looked beyond race, religion, and ethnicity. We should embrace Muslims with kindness—those who believe in the harmony of all men and women living together as equals—and pray for and forgive those who do not share this vision of unity. For the God we serve is merciful, and because He is the Creator, He looks upon us all as His children.

Jesus says, "A new commandment I give unto you, that ye love one another; as I have loved you, that ye also love one another. By this shall all men know that ye are my disciples, if ye have love one to another." He commands us time and time again as his followers to love one another, and here, I am simply reminding us of what we have been instructed to do. God did not command us to only love other Christians, Jews, Muslims, Mormons, Sikhs, Buddhists, Baha'is, Jainists, Shintoists, Rastafarians, Hindus, Taoists, Confucianists, Caodaiists, Shamans, Zoroastrians, Unitarians, Primal Indigenous, Animists, Pagans, or to hate the atheists who do not believe in Him, or the agnostics who do not recognize Him. Take time today to reach out and have the courage to show kindness to someone who is *different* from yourself—whether through a smile, a cheerful word, an exchange of ideas, or however you feel best to express it.

Kindness can be contagious, and what a beautiful world we would inhabit if we all started looking upon ourselves as collective members of the "human race."

Cousins of courage

Bravery	Tenacity
Valor	Determination
Endurance	Daring
Fortitude	

Cousins of kindness

Compassion	Comfort
Mercy	Courtesy
Love	Altruism
Respect	Empathy

CHAPTER 33
WHY WE MUST NOT GIVE UP ON BEING KIND

The easiest thing in the world to do is to quit or give up. To feel hopeless is to be helpless. To be apathetic invites the destruction of all, whether directly involved or not. Even in the biblical story of Eden, God did not give up or turn his back on Adam and Eve, although he knew they had done wrong. He made them understand that they had been disobedient and banished them from the Garden of Eden, yet continued to love his creations as a caring parent would. It would have been easy to have given them over to the devil (serpent), however, God believed in humans, and we must also.

We must continue to tear at the walls that separate us, whether it be race, color, gender, age, creed, religion, national origin, socioeconomic status, political belief, ethnicity, disability, sexual orientation, or whatever if we are to thrive as a species. Being kind to one another and accepting our differences will unite us because it is ignorance and mistrust which seek to nullify kindness. We are all interconnected—the act of one person anywhere can affect the actions of people everywhere.

This morning, while looking out of my backyard window during a blustery drab fall day, I saw a single leaf twisting in the wind. As it rocked back and forth, it caught my attention. What really made this leaf stand out was that all the other thousands of leaves on this large tree had fallen onto the ground, but this one leaf refused to fall. Instead, it made one last attempt to be relevant and remind us of the summer past just before winter's arrival. Yes, it was dead and brown and unsightly, but it stood out because of its rebellion against the status quo. It made me think if only we could be more like this leaf: to stand out and be known for our kindness and humanity—though thousands have fallen aside and not risen to their potential because they lacked the courage to say: "I may be unsightly or beautiful, poor or rich, old or young, this race or that race, prince or pauper, this political party or that political party, I refuse to give up on being kind to either friend, family or foe—and through my actions and words I will transform hearts and minds!"

The winds of resistance will always be present—sometimes strong, sometimes gentle. It is not solely how you react to these winds but that you hold onto those guiding principles that God has given to mankind—to love one another—and without fear. There will be those who will paint you as idealistic or given to fantasy; however, always remember the source of your strength—it is not man-made. If you need a reminder, read where it says in the Bible: "He who dwells in the secret place of the Most High shall abide under the shadow of the Almighty. I will say of the Lord, "He is my refuge and my fortress; My God, in Him I will trust." Surely He shall deliver you from the snare of the fowler and from the perilous pestilence. He shall cover you with His feathers, and under His wings you shall take refuge; His truth shall be your shield and buckler. You shall not be afraid of the terror by night, nor of the arrow that flies by day, nor of the pestilence that walks in darkness, nor of the destruction that lays waste at noonday. A thousand may fall at your side, and ten thousand at your right hand; but it shall not come near you."

I will always remember that one leaf that helped renew my faith and remind me of why I should dare to be different and to never give up on being kind.

CHAPTER 34

YOU CANNOT 'SAVE THE WORLD' THROUGH YOUR KINDNESS!

One common mistake that kind and nice/sincere people make is they sometimes believe they can help or change or save everyone. They go to great lengths to try to help everyone who shows a need or could use an intervention of kindness. I had previously mentioned in another chapter the altruistic and tragic sacrifices of the great scientist, Dr. George Price, as an example. I believe that you cannot help everyone effectively; you must carefully assess each situation selflessly.

Case in point, I was at a conference in Las Vegas, Nevada, and was walking to one of the local convenience stores from my hotel on the Las Vegas Strip. While on my way to the store, I came across several homeless people—each with their unique solicitation signs. One woman's sign simply said, "Homeless, please help!" as she sat by the side of the path gazing at the passersby. Another fifty feet from her location sat a man who was unkempt and unshaven; however, his sign was more provocative. It read, "Skip the BS, I need money for beer!" Then there was yet another man a little further from him. Well, I went into the store and picked up the item that I needed and headed back to my hotel. Along the way, I passed by the same homeless people whom I had previously encountered. I walked past the homeless man with the beer sign, smiled, and nodded at the homeless woman and the other man. Then farther down, I noticed a man rummaging through trash bins on the boulevard. I saw him take what appeared to be a half-eaten sandwich and hurriedly stuff it into his pocket. He did so enthusiastically, as if he had found something of high value. I thought to myself, this person could use some help; he is seeking what we all need—food! So, as I got close by, I called out to him and he spun around, startled, and defensive, with his fists raised in a fighting posture. I managed to calm him down by showing him the money that I was about to give him. He took the money, made a grunting sound, and continued with what he was doing. My assessment afterward was this man was made homeless by his mental illness or drugs and was actively searching for sustenance.

Could I have helped the other three homeless people? Perhaps, but what moved me most was witnessing someone trolling through refuse looking for food—something that many of us take for granted. Not judging the other homeless people, but he was not looking for a handout, neither was he hoping to feed an addiction or habit. He simply wanted to eat. I also realized through my brief interaction with the man that he neither knew nor understood my kind act, but that is not what was important—it was selfless and intended to help that one person who, in my opinion, expressed the greatest and most basic need. We cannot 'save the world' or help everyone, but we can try to make the world a better place and reduce suffering—one person at a time.

CHAPTER 35

KINDNESS IS LIKE A GARDEN

It is true that kindness is like a garden because it must be cultivated. As I mentioned in another chapter, I love gardening, and while I have recently learned to enjoy eating vegetables, I also like watching them grow. Gardening is like this: you prepare, or cultivate, the soil for planting, then insert and cover your seeds and ensure that there is ample water and sun. And, as a rule, you always anticipate that there will be some weeds mixed in with your crops, but you do your best to prevent them from growing and spreading.

As with kindness, we should also selflessly enjoy sowing seeds of love and helping others. Sometimes, we have an opportunity to watch someone grow because of the kindness that we have shown them, but like cultivating a garden, we should anticipate the possibility of some negativity, our act of kindness being rebuffed, or ridicule "weeds" because of our attempt to do good works. The key is not to internalize this "surface" reaction: it could be that the person has had a bad day, or is depressed because of their circumstance, or resistant to change. Continue to cultivate and sow seeds of kindness because eventually, there will be ample soil, and sun, and water where conditions will be ideal for the seed, and that is where hope and love begin to grow.

Jesus says of the valued crop and the lowly weed, "Let both grow together until the harvest: and in the time of harvest I will say to the reapers, Gather ye together first the tares, and bind them in bundles to burn them: but gather the wheat into my barn." Sometimes you will not be able to ferret out all the "weeds"—noise and negativity—as you go about spreading kindness, but keep believing that someday, when the crops are mature, there will be a harvest. Have courage; keep sowing and do not get "down in the weeds", for a barn has been prepared for what was planted and that which will be reaped.

CHAPTER 36
COURAGE OR COWARDICE?

There is a misconception that people who are kind or nice will not fight or lack the courage to. Neither is true. The reason being: Kind people do not provoke fights, are slow to anger, and are peacemakers. Kind people believe in the harmonious living of all of God's creations. Kind people do not seek to stir up conflict or strife but will work tirelessly toward a resolution. This does not mean they will put up with guff from anyone, or weakly roll over and give up when threatened. If they feel that they are in the right or defending a principle sacred to them, whoever is the initiator will be up against a very formidable adversary. It takes courage to stand up to a bully, and it takes even greater courage to walk away and avoid a fight. Walking away is not cowardice! A sincere, kind, or nice person will stand there and fight until the threat has subsided if other peaceful options, including walking away, have been exhausted.

Sometimes in Western societies, the person who wants to fight or is always willing to take on the world is idolized as being tough, macho, or a "person of action." They are looked upon or revered as being brave and confident and worthy of emulation; however, this is not always true. That person may have some underlying anger or behavioral issues, or fights to hide insecurities, or uses this method because they are not equipped to resolve issues through constructive dialogue and peaceful means. Regardless, in my opinion, this is cowardice—the use of force or intimidation exclusively in lieu of mediation. Irrationality prevails when open communication is immediately ruled out as a solution and confrontation and/or violence ensues.

The greater a person's courage, the more they will disdain violence. I equate it with a wild animal finding itself with no route of escape, so the next instinctual step for survival would be to fight. Because we are humans and God has endowed us with intellect and compassion, for us to stoop to the level of animals as our first line of defense shows insecurity and weakness. There will be times when we will be called upon to defend ourselves or our principles; however, it is the way in which we approach the situation that will determine our separation from the more animalistic instinct, which is to impulsively lash out and physically fight.

In the movies and in popular culture, the kind, humble person is sometimes portrayed as spineless, quiet, aloof, or as a weakling. The Bible says, "For the Lord takes pleasure in His people; He adorns the humble with victory." The kind and humble person will always be victorious because they are operating at a spiritual level, and because of this, God has taken special favor for "His people." When you operate in the way of the world, you miss His blessings and favor because you do not carry His teachings in your heart. The Bible also says, "Blessed are the meek: for they shall inherit the earth." So, what will the man or woman of violence or worldly action inherit? Surely, the wrath of God! So, continue to be kind, meek in spirit, and humble because it takes more courage to remain so and be victorious over the snares and ways of the world.

CHAPTER 37
CAN YOU BE TOO KIND?

This question usually accompanies those who fear being kind or thought of as a nice person. I have heard people say that when they are perceived as "nice or kind," others try to use them, and when this happens, they feel humiliated, angry, and hurt. It is partly because of this fear that they have attempted to minimize ever feeling this vulnerable again. They essentially hide their tendency toward kindness because they do not have the courage to overcome the hurt that might ensue due to "self" and internalization. Basically, these people have forgotten that one of the touchstones of kindness is forgiveness and to try not to wallow in the treacherous deeds of others.

One common thread that ran through the people who shared their stories with me was that the person causing them the greatest pain or disappointment when they felt they were being used was often a close relative they were trying to help. Kahlil Gibran says if we love someone, we should let them go, and should they come back, they always belonged to us. If not, they were never ours.

While it may be difficult to let our families, love interests, or good friends "go" entirely, we can protect ourselves from being hurt by them again by minimizing the potential for its repetition. A great deal of protection will come from not allowing yourself to get into a position where you can be used repeatedly all the while expecting a different outcome. There is a saying: The true definition of insanity is repeating the same action, over and over, hoping for a different result. This is not to say that you should never be kind to this person again; however, you should implement some checks and balances to enhance the probability of a much different, more positive outcome when new interactions are presented. Your kindness should be given selflessly, and whatever the reaction to it, do not internalize it. In my opinion, if the outcome is negative, it is okay to be disappointed because this is merely a surface emotion when compared to the deeper feeling of hurt.

When we are in relationships, or in love, the stakes can sometimes be higher because we want to be kind toward the person of our deepest affections and will sometimes do whatever it takes to hang onto them or make them happy. In return, we falsely expect respect, kindness, love, and empathy. What happens when the relationship sours because one person feels that they have given more than the other? Or if they feel they are being used, or were "too kind and accommodating?" This could lead to bitterness and an overall dissolution of the relationship because there is no longer love, kindness, or respect. Future relationships could be impacted due to the absence of the courage or resolve to give the next person this level of affection because we have been hurt or felt used in the past and are bitter. So, we guard our emotions and dole out our affections incrementally in this new relationship instead of fully committing. Do not surrender to the fear of being too kind but rise to the reality that you must always try leading with your head and not with your heart.

CHAPTER 38
HAVE YOU EVER MISSED AN OPPORTUNITY TO SHOW KINDNESS?

I think we've all been here before—where we look back or reflect deeply on an action or inaction—and wished for another chance to relive that moment all over again. Several years ago, I was leaving a home improvement store, and an elderly lady was in the car ahead of me. The street she was about to pull out onto was treacherous because there were no immediate traffic lights around to slow down oncoming cars so that one could safely pull out. The traffic began to clear just a bit, and the woman thought it was okay to go. Then suddenly, from across the street, another driver sped out, going in the opposite direction, hitting her car, tearing off the front bumper, damaging its hood and other components. The other car came across the lanes so fast that it was a blur. I waited to make sure that the impact did not hurt the woman, then she emerged from the car unharmed, just a bit shaken. So, I sat there for a moment, then backed up and went slowly down another driveway away from the accident. Through my rearview mirror, I could see her standing outside the crumpled car.

As she stood there alone, she looked so embarrassed, with her head bowed while the chartreuse-green antifreeze and obsidian-black oil seeped slowly from underneath her car and into the street. I had someplace else to go before heading home but momentarily thought to myself, "Maybe you should turn around and stand there with her; ask her if she is okay, comfort her at least until the authorities arrive." However, I kept on driving. I was not in a hurry to get to the next store, and I did not have somewhere pressing to be afterward, so I had time. I drove on to the shop, and about an hour or so later headed home, passing the scene of the accident. The lady was gone, the mangled cars had been removed, and the shattered glass and twisted shards of metal were swept. Only the remnants of oil and antifreeze remained painted across the asphalt canvas of the road. I began to feel bad because the lady needed someone to stand there with her, and I had missed the opportunity. I wish I could go back to that day because someday, I might need someone to stand with and comfort me—for just a little while.

My late mother, years ago, shared with me her own "moment." There was a woman who lived in our neighborhood who was known to be regularly inebriated, and she would always walk past our house on her way to visit one of her relatives. I did not know her very well, but I knew her kids, and from what I knew of them, part of her drunkenness stemmed from the trouble they seemed to always find themselves in. They were not bad kids, but bad things followed them like a moth to a light bulb in the night. My mother did not drink or smoke and spent considerable time at church when she was not at work, as I had previously shared. She was known in our city block for her sense of humor, kind disposition, and friendliness. This woman somehow knew about this and out of the blue stopped by our house one day. My mother vaguely knew the woman and, though surprised to find her at our door, kindly invited her in. The woman began to bare her soul while sharing the problems that she was having and how it led to her excessive alcohol use. She reached out to my mother in the hope that she would take her under her wing and help guide and uplift her.

My mother listened to her and showed compassion in her misery, and when the lady had finished, she left. My mother and this lady never had an opportunity to sit down again and talk, and my mother always felt in retrospect that there was more that she could or should have done. She knew where the lady lived and of her relatives further down our street but never did reach out to her. For all the good that my mother did for so many people when she was alive, she always regretted this one missed opportunity to help someone in need. You and I still have an opportunity; we are alive; therefore, we have a chance to make a difference today. I am haunted by my inaction and self-centeredness toward the lady with the wrecked car, but I have grown and learned from this experience. When the next opportunity presents itself, I will do the right thing in the spirit of kindness, empathy, and compassion—I will stand up!

CHAPTER 39

TAKE TIME TO SAY, "THANK YOU", WHEN YOU ARE SHOWN KINDNESS

A s a father, I have made it a priority to raise our children to say thank you when someone does something kind or special for them. I am not old-fashioned, but I am passing along to them what my parents taught me and my siblings. Years ago, when I was a freshman in high school, our mother became very ill and spent considerable time in the hospital for observation and endured a battery of medical tests. My mother became a single parent following the early death of our father from brain cancer, so all the responsibilities of transporting and caring for us, making sure that we were clothed and fed and loved, all fell on her shoulders. She was our "superwoman" in that she was smart, had a successful career in accounting and bookkeeping, was thrifty, was an amazing chef, could create almost anything with her Singer sewing machine, and grow the most scrumptious garden produce—all while raising her three young children alone.

There was a lady who lived one street over from ours and she and her husband were good friends of the family. Upon hearing that mother was infirmed, she immediately jumped into action, asking what she could do to help. My mother told her the only thing that she was not able to do was to take my brother and me to school. Every day our neighbor would drive up to our home early in the morning to pick us up and take us to school, and she made us feel special and loved, knowing that we were worried about our mother's health. She did this for over a month until my mother was well enough to resume taking us to school. I will never forget this woman's kindness.

Whenever I saw her, I thanked her. Every Christmas holiday, I would, at a minimum, send a card thanking her. When she became elderly and was in a nursing home, I would stop by to visit, to hug and tell her, "Thank you." She passed away not very long ago, and I will always remember her for her kindness. Over the span of decades, I have remained humbled by the great example she set for me.

CHAPTER 40

PERHAPS SOME OF THE GREATEST EXAMPLES OF COURAGE AND KINDNESS

Most people have read, heard, or seen the movie of the courageously touching story, *The Diary of Anne Frank*. During the Nazi occupation of the Netherlands, there were laws prohibiting anyone from helping Jews, and should they get caught, they faced incarceration, deportation, or execution. The former employees of Anne Frank's father, Otto, upon hearing the Nazis were moving into their country, knew it would mean sudden death for the Frank family. The Frank family and Otto had always been kind and welcoming to the employees, so they courageously hid the family and others, risking their freedom and lives in an act of defiance.

History teaches us that there have been many heroic stories, known and not so well-known, where people risked their lives, and freedom, or through truly altruistic actions, selflessly eased the suffering of others. During slavery in North America, there were countless people—enslaved and free blacks, American Indians, and people of different religious and ethnic groups who would ferry slaves across rivers, hide them in their barns, and feed and clothe them during their passage on the Underground

Railroad to freedom. Some were prominent people in their communities and had they been discovered helping slaves to escape, could have lost everything, or faced prison. These courageous individuals did not have to help the slaves, they could have ignored their plight, or become some of the very people who hunted them, but they had a conscience, and they knew they had a duty to do what was right. These are the highest examples of benevolence, courage, and kindness, and there are many, many others. It gives me pause because if it were you or I that needed to hide the Frank family, or the slaves, would we risk it all to help them? Would we have the courage or compassion to defy that which was morally wrong by doing the right thing?

CHAPTER 41
WHEN KIND ACTS BEGET KINDNESS IN RETURN

I have said repeatedly throughout the book how we are to perform our kind acts selflessly and expect nothing in return. However, there will be times when someone will become so moved by our kindness, they will begin and continue to heap good deeds upon us. About fifteen years ago, during the month of September, my wife was leaving home to run an errand. As she was driving down our road, she just happened to look in the direction of a house that sat far off where an elderly woman lived alone. It was dusk, and my wife could barely make out a figure wriggling around on the ground.

We live in a semirural area, and the houses have large spaces between them, so it is not uncommon for someone or something to not be seen from our road. My wife, knowing that this lady lived alone, backed up her car and pulled into her long driveway. As she approached the house, she could see that it was the elderly lady lying on the ground trying to get up, so my wife jumped out of the car and ran toward her to help. The lady had been standing on a small step ladder washing the windows of her home when it gave way, sending her crashing to the ground. My wife asked the lady if she was okay. The lady said yes and motioned to my wife to pull her into the house. My wife, a Registered Nurse, looked her over to make sure that nothing was broken during her fall but did not do as she had asked and instead called for an ambulance. The woman did not want to draw attention to her mishap, and since she lived alone and was in her nineties, she feared that her relatives might decide that she could no longer live independently and would force her to move into a nursing home. So, my wife stayed and comforted her until they were joined by a neighbor across the road, who kept an eye on the elderly lady. He had been alerted when he saw my wife's car in the driveway and its lights. My wife told the neighbor that she had called for an ambulance, and he said he would stay with her until it arrived.

About a week later, a man knocked on our door and introduced himself as the elderly lady's son. He proceeded to thank my wife most sincerely for helping his mother and for caring for her after her tumble from the ladder. My wife told him it was a miracle that she was able to see his mother at all because it had gotten so dark. I truly believe had my wife not driven by the house when she did, the lady could have been left lying there exposed well into the increasingly cold night.

The following winter brought some sizable snow accumulations, and one day I went outside to shovel it. To my surprise, our driveway had been cleared. I had not hired a snowplow driver, but there it was, perfectly plowed! This went on for a while, and then one day, after a fresh blast of snow, I again went outside to shovel and saw a pickup truck with a blade on its front coming up the driveway. As the truck got closer, a friendly white-haired man leaned out the window, smiled, and mouthed the word, "Hi!" while waving. I initially searched in vain for a reference as to who he was; then it came to me—it was the son of the elderly lady! He pulled up beside me and began to tell me about growing up in his mother's house. The more he spoke, the more I could tell that he deeply loved and adored his mother. He then did a half-wave, rolled up the window, and went about clearing the drive. Afterward, I thanked him profusely and told him that what my wife did for his mother, she would have done for anyone. I did not want him to feel obligated to shovel my driveway each time it snowed. He smiled, shook my hand, and said, "I'm sure she would have; tell your wife I said, 'Hi!'" For many winters, even years after his mother passed, when it snows, he still comes by to help us. We call him our "snow angel" because we only see him during the winter months, and his kindness continues to bring warmth to the season.

CHAPTER 42
KINDNESS AND RELIGION

First, I am a Christian and, as such, can only write from this perspective. I respect other religions and feel there is a universality that flows through them all in that our actions and behaviors should reflect what we believe. Although most religions consider kindness to be one of the highest virtues to practice, we sometimes find ourselves, or members of our churches, temples, synagogues, mosques, halls, meeting houses, and gurdwaras, doing just the opposite. All the pettiness, worldly politics, tattling, meanness, and gossip are brought into the very place where this destructive behavior should be prayed for or meditated on for redemptive purposes. If we do not separate ourselves from displaying those things found outside of our religious institutions, we cheapen our beliefs.

Like you, I have heard countless times where someone—both follower and non-follower—will say: "I don't attend this or that place of worship because I don't see any difference in what they do there than what I see every day out in the world." Or "They were not very friendly or kind," or, "I never feel welcomed at such or such institutions." How can we change this? How can we be different from that which is found in the world? By trying to live an exemplary, not perfect, life and conduct ourselves in such a way that it becomes apparent that we stand out from others in "the world." This sometimes makes people curious because they will want to know more about you, where you worship, and what you believe.

The adage that talk is cheap is applicable here. Some people talk a good game or come across as virtuous, but their actions betray the very words they say, like the kind/phony person. Having discernment will also help cut through the false images of goodness some people will try to portray. When you go into your religious institutions, leave the earthly world behind, for it is not the same as the spiritual world. When you commune with God, the Creator, you are operating at the highest level in the universe, and it is at this level where lives are forever changed, and miracles do happen. You cannot expect change or spiritual enhancement or modification when you operate through the world, because the world is finite and God infinite, thus, the universe. Be known for your integrity, kindness, compassion, and morals.

CHAPTER 43
IT TAKES COURAGE TO BE KIND WHEN WE ARE HURTING

Think back to your most painful moment; it could have been an injury, heartbreak, an illness, or any number of things. If you can remember how you felt, then you know it was not pleasant. Being kind is the last thing on our minds when we are hurt—we just want some relief, or an intervention that will take away the pain. You may have gone through a divorce or broken up with your boyfriend or girlfriend, maybe you lost a loved one, or you lost the job you depended on to feed and clothe your family. Maybe your child is in trouble or the person you thought was your good friend and confidant turned on you. Any of these and more could be reasons for our not wanting to feel too generous with our kindness. I bring all of this to your attention because it is alright to feel this way; we are only human. What is not alright is to take this pain and pass it on to someone else because you want them to also feel or feed your pain.

We all have had our painful experiences—some over many years—and we must try to pray and work through these, but not at the expense of someone else's joy. As mentioned previously, Eckhart Tolle, in his book *"A New Earth: Awaken Your Life's*

Purpose," calls this emotional pain the "pain-body." Tolle basically describes the "pain-body" as an accumulation of negative energy, or pain, stored in our minds over time. There are "triggers" – people, memories, events, bitterness, etc. – that can summon these negative feelings, where unconsciously and subconsciously the pain activates and affects our moods, thoughts, and behaviors.

Years ago, I remember reading where Les Brown, the popular motivational speaker, said whenever you get knocked down in life, land on your back. If you can look up, you can get up. It takes courage to rebound when life deals you a blow and even more courage to be kind while you go through the pain during this time. Most people have had at least a glancing moment's thought about suicide due to feeling the pain was too great; however, very few of us take this lethal leap. It is during this time you feel severely apathetic and that whatever "it" is, it is not going to get much better. This condition could either derive from a lack of faith, mental illness, or both. I recently learned of an acquaintance's suicide. He was an outwardly friendly and kind person—always upbeat, so when I heard of his passing, it caught me totally off-guard.

What was even more troubling about his suicide were the many accolades given to him, posthumously, about his character, helping spirit, and loving family. Perhaps he never knew how much he was loved, so take the time today to tell someone they are special and loved—while they are here.

God gives us only so many days on this Earth; some good, some bad. Make the best of the good days you are given; know there will be some bad days, too. As much as possible, try to be kind, even when you are hurting, because that person who you might inflict your pain on only has so much time here and so many good days, as well. Do not rob them of the good days they are given in exchange for your bad days. Pray and ask for the strength and courage to work through your pain. Know that "to everything there is a season, and a time to every purpose" and better days are ahead. It will take faith or, perhaps, added counseling. Try to believe or seek help—but hold on!

CHAPTER 44
KINDNESS: YOUR KIDS AND YOUR PARENTS

The most influential people in your life will most likely be your mother or father, or both. They are usually the first beings with whom we interact soon after being born. This is not always the case, as I have mentioned before. Some of us were born into the world without either parents being present or involved in our lives thereafter. For those whose parents were there, they carry a lot of influence. I was fortunate in that I had both a mother and a father in my early life and through them, I learned how to care, how to eat, how to live, and how to love. You may be a parent, or you have one.

If you are a parent, like I am, you know about sacrifice. You know about raising children to become responsible adults, good people, and followers of God's word. You know about the heartache and disappointment that comes when they forget the numerous teachings and examples you tried to instill in them. Through both joy and pain, you love them—unconditionally.

Above all else, be kind to your children, and respect and encourage them when they are being honest with you. They are watching you, and whether you agree with this or not, they will more than likely imitate what they see you do, or not do. Keep your promises and be truthful with them. Likewise, children, respect, be truthful, and be kind to your parents. They may be elderly, or perhaps were not the "best parents" or examples to follow while growing up, but they are your parents and, as such, a part of you. The Bible instructs us to "Honour thy father and mother," and unless they were "instructing" you to do evil, you are to respect their teachings.

Few things trouble me more than when I see or hear about a parent mistreating their children, or a person abusing their parents—especially if they are elderly. The news media is full of stories of children hurting parents and parents harming children. Where does this depth of anger and depravity come from to morph into someone's death? That person who should have had a special place in our lives, we destroy. Parents do not mistreat your children; be kind to them—they are a gift to you—and you are blessed to have each other.

CHAPTER 45
EXCUSES FOR NOT SHOWING KINDNESS

"He'll never change, so why should I help him?"
"I never liked '_____' people—period!"
"It's not my problem, why should I get involved?"

We all have them or have encountered them at one time or another; some random excuse for not helping someone or not wanting to get involved, and at the time, it seemed rational enough to justify our action or inaction. When we can minimize human suffering, what else will we minimize? Will we minimize homicide, or rape, or persecution, or addiction? Are these "okay" too just because they may not impact us directly? What if it was our child, brother or sister, mother or father, wife, husband, or significant other; would it be acceptable if any of these maladies befell them? No! When we consciously or subconsciously allow our ego to enter our feelings toward others in need, it is almost as if we are observers of an event rather than participants. Being an observer is easy because it takes no effort to sit back and watch someone's demise or problems from a distance, so we become emotionally detached from the person or situation. It then becomes easy to conjure up reasons to be apathetic. Maybe this has happened or is happening to you.

Kindness is void of ego; it is about the "you" that can become a "participant" and help make a difference. Check your ego, because the greater it becomes, the less effective in helping others you become. It takes courage to overcome or master the ego and even more to put it in its place whenever it rears its "self-centered" head.

CHAPTER 46
KINDNESS AND OUR ENEMIES

For me, this is the most challenging thing to do: to engage my enemies. This is a developmental area that I need to work on, and it ranks at the very top. It takes great courage to walk amongst your enemies and show kindness, knowing that they hate you. I would dare say that this could probably be the most challenging thing you will ever do if you love kindness. Jesus said, "Love your enemies, bless them that curse you, do good to them that hate you, and pray for them which despitefully use you, and persecute you." Here is someone who has it out for you, and you are instructed to love them? We have all had enemies in our lives—those who disliked us, or we them, sometimes without provocation, or due to jealousy or envy, and so on.

Our enemies go by different names: haters, adversaries, opponents, foes, rivals, nemesis, etc., and they all have one common thread—they do not like us. Fortunate, and rare, is the person who has not had any enemies in life, but if they live long enough, they will. It is written that if we fear the Lord, we will have His protection. The Bible bears this out with these words: "Though I walk in the midst of trouble, thou wilt revive me: thou shalt stretch forth thine hand against the wrath of mine enemies, and thy right hand shall save me." So, why should we be afraid of our enemies? Why should we not have the courage to be kind to them when the Lord says He has our backs? I do not think we are being told to walk into danger, but we are also not instructed to flee either; only to turn the other cheek should someone "smite" us. That is where having faith, doing right, and following Jesus's example should take place.

If you follow the movies and television shows, you may be led to believe that the only way to deal with one's enemies is to eliminate them. We have all wished that somehow those who we consider our nemesis would simply disappear. Here was something revolutionary, however, —love them! I am sure that when these words first fell on the ears of the listeners during Jesus's Sermon on the Mount, they surely thought him insane or suicidal for saying this. Jesus, however, had something altogether different in mind in that he believed if we could love our enemies and show kindness, it would shame or pain them into reconsidering their negative attitude toward us. The Bible says, "Therefore, if thine enemy hunger, feed him; if he thirst, give him drink: for in so doing thou shalt heap coals of fire on his head." I will continue to pray and work on this. How about you?

CHAPTER 47
KINDNESS AND FRIENDS

"A true friend will love us, challenge us to be our best and, above all else, remind us to be merciful." ~ J. Touché

Our friends are second only to our families in terms of playing an influential role in our development, outlook, and thinking. That is why we must be selective and wise in how we choose our friends. Sometimes we do not have a say in how we find our friends; they find us, but they must want to be our friends for the right reasons and should be of good character. For the most part, we become friends because we see something in that person that we admire or bond with. Perhaps we grew up with them, they are good athletes, great students, exceptional conversationalists, or share similar interests. Then there are the other, more fleeting, or pseudo reasons, such as being popular, cool, attractive, dangerous, edgy, hot, and more.

The one consistent thing that you will notice in our interactions with our friends, for the most part, is that we are kind or good to them. We sometimes go to great lengths to not offend them, and when they are doing wrong, we turn a blind eye. So, the question is: What kind of friend are you? If you are truly someone's friend, you should be kind to them, of course, but you should also have the courage to speak out if you see them doing things with which you do not agree. Too many times, because we are afraid of losing our friends, we will coddle and protect them, even when we know they are wrong. In my opinion, a friend is not only someone around whom you can be yourself but also someone who, if they are the right person, can help make you a better person – iron sharpening iron. We also should not judge our friends; however, when there is a pattern of wrongdoing, we should question whether to remain friends with that person.

If you see your friend heading down the wrong path, be kind and truthful with them. First, let them know that you care about them, then express how you feel and what impact their actions are having or could have on the future of your relationship. Do not try to change your friends, only their way of thinking. If you continue to be uncomfortable with their actions and behaviors, then it may be time to move away from them. Have the courage to decide whether you should remain friends or have them in your life at all. The mistake too many of us make is that we hold on to someone long after the relationship has stopped growing. You must remember that God sometimes puts people in our lives for only a season, and then it is time to move on because you have gained all there is to learn from them and vice versa. When this happens, others will enter your life, and your growth will continue anew.

CHAPTER 48
KINDNESS AND FORGIVENESS

Second only to being kind to our enemies, another difficult thing, in my opinion, would be forgiving those who have hurt or wronged us. We have all felt the pain of being hurt, and it sometimes feels like an ache if it is prolonged. When it is present, it bothers us, but it does not have the same intensity as it did when the hurt first occurred. We sometimes carry this ache around because we have not yet forgiven the person who caused the pain or circumstance. We have not mustered up the courage to look at this ache head on and say to it, "You have no power over me; I will not carry you around anymore!" There are people who have decades of pain within them, and there are studies that suggest mental anguish and pain can manifest into physical pain and disability over time. That is why we must work our way through it. You can start by praying on it; pray for the person who caused the pain and pray for the strength and courage to overcome it.

How can we be kind to or forgive someone who has caused us pain and hurt, you may ask? It will not be easy, and unfortunately, because many people think of being kind as a sign of weakness, we will present a toughened, stony disposition toward this person. We will dislike or avoid them altogether because we do not want to get hurt again. What this then becomes is what I described in the chapter on bitterness—it is the enemy of kindness because bitterness can destroy our empathy and compassion. We have a choice here: Become bitter or become better by practicing forgiveness.

Do not let anyone take away your capacity to show kindness. Kindness begets mercy, and when you are merciful, it is a gift from God. We have all fallen short of His grace, and it probably pained God when we did not follow His will, but He forgave us! He allowed us to live and prosper on the land that He provided. Had He been a vengeful God, we would have surely met with death upon our first infraction. That is why we must practice forgiveness, learn from our past, and continue to be kind to everyone — especially to those who have hurt us. The person who hurt us may see our strength in that we have not been crushed by their offense, or gave way to becoming vindictive or hating them, and take notice. They might even feel remorse for what they have done to us. There is power in "letting go" and moving on. Life is too short to carry long grudges—let go and let God!

Lastly, do not allow yourself to get in a position where you could get hurt by that person again. There are warning signs along the way, and we must be able to, through our five senses, faith, and discernment, read and adhere to those signals.

CHAPTER 49
WHY RANDOM ACTS OF KINDNESS SHOULD START AT HOME

We have all seen or experienced it ourselves: kids talking back to parents, husbands, or significant others mistreating their wives or lovers, lovers or wives berating their husbands or significant others, parents disrespecting their kids, family members abusing their pets, and so on. Try being kind to your spouse, your significant other, your kids, your parents, and your pets. Kindness is love in action. Your words may not outlive your actions; however, the feelings that you leave with people can last a lifetime.

While growing up, I never once heard my mother tell me she loved me—her kind actions, however, spoke of her deep love for me—and I felt loved! Do nice things for a family member today; take your pet out for a walk at its favorite park, prepare a special meal for your family, and dine together, take your wife or husband or friend on a date because kindness starts where you live. You cannot truly promote kindness if your house is full of anger, disarray, conflict, or strife. Kindness incubates best where there is love and peace. Then take this kindness beyond your four walls and share it both randomly and purposely with others, knowing that when you return home, love will greet you at the door. Love is the catalyst of kindness, and it transforms all that it touches.

CHAPTER 50
KINDNESS AND OUR NEIGHBORS

Our neighbors may be alike or different from us, and we must all find a way to get along. You have seen or heard of neighbors feuding, and to this point, I need only to mention the legendary and deadly struggles between two American families—the Hatfields and the McCoys. We need to find a way to live together as harmoniously as possible. Your neighbors are not all going to be the friendly, warm, fuzzy, waving type, and some might not say anything to you at all, but you must accept them as they are. If you feel you want to "kill" your neighbor, kill them with kindness. Kindness is the universal expression of love, which can lead to the undoing of violence.

Years ago, we lived in a suburb of St. Paul, Minnesota, in a townhouse. As you know, they are attached, so you will more than likely see or hear your neighbor at some time. The latter was our case. Adjacent to our place was the home of a young man in his late teens who did not work but was a drummer in a band. He and his band used the garage as a "band shell" because it would be empty when his mother would take the car out and go to work. And, yes, it did echo—terribly so! I am a lover of many genres of music, and I can honestly say that what they were playing was not music. If I could place the music, it would be close to a bizarre form of alternative rock, and the band should have continued to search for an "alternative" to that. It had no beat, no structure, and it was LOUD!

At that time, my wife worked the midnight shift at a university-owned hospital in Minneapolis. So, after a night of helping patients and related duties, she would come home around eight in the morning, and just as she had started to doze off, about an hour and a half later, the band would kick it into high gear. I knew my wife was sleep-deprived, and she would tell me so. After weeks of this "noise," I went over and asked the guy respectfully to turn down the volume on his speakers. He nodded, but it was so slight that I did not know whether it meant "yes" or just an acknowledgment that I had said something. Well, after about a week or so of diminished noise, it started blasting again. I knew some of my other neighbors, and when I approached them about the "noise," I would ask whether the music had affected them as it had me. For the most part, the neighbors did agree that it was way too loud, and one even told me, to my chagrin, "Well, I would rather he and his buddies play their music loud than break into our homes." I still question his logic to this day, but anyway, I was forced to talk to his mother.

His mother was a very sweet lady, and she worked all the time, so during one of those rare moments when she was home, I went over and calmly explained the situation. I literally "killed" her with kindness, and the more I shared how my wife was a nurse who was on the midnight shift and was not getting much sleep because of the "band," the more empathetic she became and promised me that she would talk to her son. It was not quite "the day the music died," but it was a lot more palatable after that. The point is that you must respect and be kind to your neighbors, even if they are not agreeable because at the end of the day, you are still going to be living next to or near them.

If you have something to say about an infringement on your property, or "ears" as in my case, have the courage to approach them about it—do not sit there in silent suffering—letting things escalate to your boiling point. Above all else, drop the attitude and be courteous, warm, and kind when you do; they might be more accommodating toward what you are asking. In our case, within a few months, we moved from our townhouse to where we currently live—with ample distance between the homes. We have that young man to thank for being the motivation behind our living a good way away from our neighbors and for never encouraging our children to play the drums.

CHAPTER 51
THE MANY FACES OF KINDNESS

Kindness comes in many colors, shapes, and sizes. It could be the young girl playing up the street, the homeless man, the woman living in the mansion, or the guy who repairs your roof. You will not always know immediately who kind is, but you will be able to tell — by their words and behaviors. The true intentions of the people behind the kindness will be revealed through their actions. Do not prejudge someone because of how they look, how they are dressed, or where they come from or live because kindness does not always manifest itself in visible things. Sometimes it is cloaked behind what we see with our eyes, and if we only look for kindness in a physical sense, we may miss it in its abstract form.

A profound example of this prejudice occurred when Jesus was introduced to Nathanael by Philip: "Philip findeth Nathanael, and saith unto him, We have found him, of whom Moses in the law, and the prophets, did write, Jesus of Nazareth, the son of Joseph. And Nathanael said unto him, can there any good thing come out of Nazareth? Philip saith unto him, come and see." Basically, Nathanael doubted that Jesus being the Messiah could come from Nazareth. Only when Jesus told him something that only the Messiah would know, did he believe.

We all have these preconceived notions about what kind people look like—either consciously or subconsciously. Because of this, we will treat the person accordingly. If they look "presentable" or "approachable," we tend to give them the respect we feel they deserve. But if they look grungy or disheveled, we are more apt to avoid them or look down our noses at them. We are all biased, to some degree, and must consciously and consistently fight this "divider" or miss out on the kindness which we cannot see with our eyes and only visible through our hearts.

I remember long ago being told that everyone should be treated the same because God sometimes sends down his angels disguised as humans to test our humanity. It made me think: What if I were to mistreat one of his messengers? I do believe there are "angels" who walk amongst and watch over us, so we should be kind to everyone—regardless of how they appear—because it is the right thing to do.

"Our prejudices cloud the beauty behind the things we see."
~ J. Touché

CHAPTER 52
KINDNESS AND COMMUNITY

We are a village within a village, and as a village, we must try to do our best to promote the good of all—especially the children. If a link is corrupt, the entire chain fails; if we fail to lift others through kindness, love, and respect, the whole planet is doomed. I, like so many of you, used to think that what happens on the other side of the world, if not the street, had no direct bearing on me. Then I looked at how my actions or inactions and those of others had a far greater impact than ever imagined.

Children are like sponges, and they will imitate the behaviors they see or experience growing up. If a child grows up in a violent environment, there is a strong probability it will also embrace violence as an outward means of expression. Whether it is the impoverished child from inner-city America who kills to survive; the privileged, yet neglected, child of well-to-do suburban parents who goes into a school and kills others; or those growing up in war-torn nations witnessing death daily, the die is cast, and these children will see violence as a means of resolution, or way of life. Their reaction is one of extreme pain. Deep down inside they cry out in protest to the world that they were robbed of their childhood due to war, neglect, or their environment, so survival and killing became their persistent reality. We are a village. If we do not have some form of positive intervention for these children, they could very well become tomorrow's criminals, terrorists, or murderers. You might ask: "What can I do to help from where I live?" You can find organizations that are involved in helping these kids, or the communities in which they reside.

I once sponsored a child through a well-known international agency, and I did it for the reasons listed above among others, but mostly out of love and concern. To be honest, there was also an element of guilt in the fact that I was fortunate to be born in one of the richest countries on Earth, just the opposite of many of those needing my help. The boy was from an impoverished African nation, and something about his eyes in the photograph the agency sent me captured my attention. I wondered, besides the persistent specter of hunger, or having to drink from and bathe in the same water, or living in absolute squalor, what else had those eyes seen? Perhaps death, disease, murder, rape, torture, war, abandonment, or more. The bigger question arose: "What will happen to him?" The answer: What happens to him may someday impact me or others in some manner. We need to have the courage and compassion to support our villages; as the link goes, so goes the chain.

IN CONCLUSION

You are wonderfully made and were given many talents and gifts. Some are meant to create, to dance, to sing, to write, to paint, to be good parents, nurses, lawyers, social workers, doctors, teachers, administrative assistants, ministers, priests, rabbis, imams, husbands and wives, scientists, salespeople, factory workers, politicians, executives, entrepreneurs, mentors, sanitation engineers, and much more. We are complex creatures and are in no way one-dimensional, so within these talents and gifts are even more talents and gifts. The question that is before you are: What will you do with this genius, and how will you use it to make the world better?

We have all been given a certain length of time to be here, and our "clock" toward our end started ticking soon after we drew our first breath. Within this time, however long or short, may we all have an opportunity to make our lives significant and try to make a difference in the lives of others. I truly believe that a big step in this direction is through seeking the courage to be kind.

I challenge you to seize the day— "carpe diem" —and cram whatever virtues there are within that 24-hour space, then watch what happens. When you sow the seeds of love and kindness, you will see those around you flourish because goodness is contagious. Dare to be different while making a difference, and always remember: You represent a far greater power than any that can ever rise against you in this world! Kind and nice/sincere guys and girls do not finish last, but they are shown mercy and grace that will sustain them to "finish" honorably and look back upon "the race in life" not as one of competition or winning, where they were out to defeat others, but as an opportunity to change lives and challenge the status quo along their journey. With this, I leave you a poem:

SEEK THE COURAGE TO BE KIND

Seek the courage to be kind; to help someone in need,
And leave behind the vanity and relentless pursuit of greed.
Where we can give a "broken" man—
the love we all have within—
Then bend or stoop to lift him up and show him how to win.
It matters not the wealth one has, or the things
some consider grand,
Or, where we work or socialize, but whether we have a plan.
To bring about true happiness and respect for those we meet
And, to make our lives more purposeful; if,
but sharing what we eat.
To strive to serve our fellow man, to be at peace with God,
And live each day to be our best—
until shrouded to meet the sod.
So, let us scale the highest mount and shout
with one voice aloud:
This day, this hour, this minute, this second—
uplift hearts with heads unbowed!
~J. Touché

Find your "Voice"—Seek the Courage to be Kind!

NOTES

Chapter 2
Cambridge Dictionary
Merriam-Webster Dictionary

Chapter 3
Cambridge Dictionary
Merriam-Webster Dictionary

Chapter 6
Goleman, Daniel, *Emotional Intelligence: Why It Can Matter More Than IQ*
Luke 10:30-35 (King James Version)
Ephesians 4:28 (King James Version)
Treves, Sir Frederick, 1st Baronet, *The Elephant Man and Other Reminiscences*, January 1923

Chapter 10
Tolle, Eckart, *A New Earth: Awakening to Your Life's Purpose*
Dickens, Charles, *A Christmas Carol*

Chapter 13
Prochaska, James O., PhD, and DiClemente, Carlo C., PhD
Transtheoretical Model of Behavior Change

Chapter 15
Keltner, Dacher, PhD, Co-Director of the Greater Good Science Center,
University of California, Berkeley

Chapter 16
Shelley, Mary Wollstonecraft, *Frankenstein; or The Modern Prometheus*
Animal Legal Defense Fund (aldf.org)

Chapter 18
Matthew 6:24 (King James Version)

Chapter 20
Matthew 10:16 (King James Version)

Chapter 21
Wikipedia, Dr. George Price

Chapter 23
1 Kings 22:20-23 (King James Version)

Chapter 27
www.worldometers.com
www.tradingeconomics.com

Chapter 30
www.cdc.gov

Chapter 32
Islamic Networks Group (www.ing.org)
John 13:34-35 (King James Version)

Chapter 33
Psalms 91 (King James Version)

Chapter 35
Matthew 13:30 (King James Version)

Chapter 36
Psalm 149:4 (King James Version)
Matthew 5:5 (King James Version)

Chapter 40
nps.gov

Chapter 43
Ecclesiastes 3:1 – 8 (King James Version)
Tolle, *Eckhart, A New Earth: Awakening to Your Life's Purpose*

Chapter 44
Exodus 20:12 (King James Version)

Chapter 46
Matthew 5:44 (King James Version)
Romans 12:20 (King James Version)
Psalms 138: 7 (King James Version)

Chapter 51
John 1:45 – 46 (King James Version)

ABOUT THE AUTHOR

J. Touché is a student of life who has always struggled with the concept of kindness—what it is and what it is not. Through extensive research and reading other books and articles about kindness, J. Touché discovered people downplayed or did not mention the courage that always accompanies sincere kindness. His first encounter with kindness was through his late mother and it intrigued him what the essence of her kindness was and discovering how courageous she really was. Having traveled to many destinations worldwide and throughout the U.S., he found that kindness is universal, and people everywhere attempted to understand it. His book results from his journey to seek sincere kindness, kind people and their motivations, self-reflection, and personal encounters that changed the course of his life. The Courage to Be Kind is about sincerity, kindness, niceness, courage, faith, prayer, selflessness, love, humanity, hope, and the core of kindness. **GOD.**

www.ingramcontent.com/pod-product-compliance
Lightning Source LLC
Chambersburg PA
CBHW050246010526
44107CB00003B/208